**CONCISE
LINCOLN
LIBRARY**

—

EDITED BY RICHARD W. ETULAIN
AND SYLVIA FRANK RODRIGUE

JASON EMERSON

Lincoln the Inventor

Southern Illinois University Press
Carbondale

Southern Illinois University Press
www.siupress.com

25 24 23 22   4 3 2 1

The Concise Lincoln Library has been made possible in part through
a generous donation by the Leland E. and LaRita R. Boren Trust.

Volumes in this series have been published with support from the
Abraham Lincoln Bicentennial Foundation, dedicated to perpetuat-
ing and expanding Lincoln's vision for America and completing
America's unfinished work.

Cover illustration adapted from a painting by Wendy Allen

Frontispiece: In preparing his application in 1849 to patent his
invention of a device to buoy vessels over shoals, Abraham Lincoln
worked with a local mechanic to build an eighteen-inch model of a
ship fitted with his contraption. Lincoln hand-carved some of the
model himself with his pocketknife. Illustration by Lloyd Ostendorf,
author of *Abraham Lincoln: The Boy, the Man*, reproduced courtesy
of publisher Phil Wagner, Springfield, Illinois, www.abelincoln.com.

The Library of Congress has cataloged the 2009 hardcover, paper-
back, and e-book editions as follows:
ISBN 978-0-8093-2898-7 (cloth)
ISBN 978-0-8093-2897-0 (paperback)
ISBN 978-0-8093-8671-0 (ebook)

Library of Congress Cataloging-in-Publication Data
Names: Emerson, Jason, 1975– author.
Title: Lincoln the inventor / Jason Emerson.
Description: Carbondale : Southern Illinois University Press,
    [2022] | Series: Concise Lincoln library | Includes bibliographical
    references and index.
Identifiers: LCCN 2021056000 (print)
    | LCCN 2021056001 (ebook) | ISBN 9780809338818 (paperback)
    | ISBN 9780809338825 (ebook)
Subjects: LCSH: Lincoln, Abraham, 1809-1865. | Presidents—United
    States—Biography. | Inventors—United States—Biography.
    | River boats—Patents—History—19th century.
Classification: LCC E457.2 .E48 2022 (print) | LCC E457.2 (ebook)
    | DDC 973.7092 [B]—dc23/eng/20211119
LC record available at https://lccn.loc.gov/2021056000
LC ebook record available at https://lccn.loc.gov/2021056001

Printed on recycled paper

SIU
Southern Illinois University System

For my daughter Olivia
who plans to be an inventor, a scientist, a chef, and
a writer when she grows up. You can do anything
and everything you choose to do, Berry, just like
Abraham Lincoln.

CONTENTS

ILLUSTRATIONS

PREFACE

This is an unconventional book. It's really an extended monograph in two sections rather than a typical book with numerous
chapters. The reason is that this is simply what the book had to be. All
artists say that creations have their own lives, their own directions.
Michelangelo said he did not create his sculpture of David, but rather
he freed the previously existing figure from the stone. Similarly, this
book—the idea of which began as an article for a children's history
magazine—took hold of me from the beginning and guided me not
so much to create it but to reveal it.

The topic of Abraham Lincoln's mechanical mind and the complete
story of his invention and patent have never been thoroughly examined.
This surprised me, for the depth of Lincoln's scientific thinking—which
reached a physical pinnacle by inventing a tangible machine—pervaded
his entire life and contributed in no small way to his greatness as man
and president. His invention of "a device to buoy vessels over shoals"
has been nominally mentioned numerous times in biographies, as has
his patent; and his lecture on "Discoveries and Inventions" actually
has been given some serious and impressive critical analyses. The more
I researched, however, the more unknown and unpublished primary
materials I continued to discover about this topic, and the more I
began to see that to consider all of Lincoln's mechanical inclinations
and accomplishments under a new light and from a new angle allows
a fresh insight into the overall character of this incomparable man.

I find it ironic that this work, the first complete consideration
of a topic so long overlooked, began as a whim to simply produce

something short and marketable for a kids' magazine. As I researched, I realized this subject could be a valuable contribution to the field of scholarly Lincoln studies. So I wrote it as a scholarly article, which was accepted for publication in the *Journal of the Illinois State Historical Society*, although it was never published. The problem, however, as probably all historians know and have experienced, was that after I submitted the article, I continued to find more evidence related to this topic.

I decided to augment the original essay and self-publish the longer version as a thirty-or-so-page monograph. I added Lincoln's patent application as an appendix and then the full transcription of his lecture on "Discoveries and Inventions" as a second appendix. With the endnotes, bibliography, illustrations, title page, acknowledgments, and the like, I suddenly found myself with an eighty-five-page manuscript. That was too long for a monograph but too short for a book. Fate then smiled upon me in subsequent research at the Library of Congress, when I found a series of correspondence between Lincoln's son Robert T. Lincoln and Lincoln's presidential secretary John G. Nicolay concerning a currently unknown edition of Abraham Lincoln's lecture and how Robert lost it and was trying to find it. Of course, I had to write that story, putting it within the context of the history of the physical pages of Lincoln's speech, as well as a brief history of the creation, delivery, and reputation of the lecture. This new section, which is chapter 2, not only revealed and examined a previously unknown piece of history but also increased the size of my monograph to its present form.

I have always enjoyed and admired short works; they get straight to the meat of a subject, without extraneous rhetoric and verbiage. While relatively uncommon today, such diminutive books often were done in the late nineteenth and early twentieth centuries, usually as personal recollections, and in the Lincoln field, I can name many that I have found valuable, one of my favorites being Julia Taft Bayne's eighty-five-page work, *Tad Lincoln's Father*. Another great little book is Jacques Barzun's fifty-page *Lincoln the Literary Genius*, a part of which I quote in the present work. The practice of publishing (often self-publishing) even shorter works—monographs—on specific topics of Lincoln's life also was a popular practice back in the early twentieth century. Historian William H. Townsend published a number of monographs on his topics of specialty, the Lincolns in Kentucky and the Todd and Helm families; Wayne C. Temple, that dean of Lincoln scholars, has published numerous impressive and valuable monographs, one of which I used for the present work.

The publication of short books and monographs has lessened extensively in recent years, which I find disappointing. The page count of a work should have no impact on its overall historical, literary, or pedagogical value. Every generation offers new interpretations of history. Not all topics can be encyclopedic, and not all publications can be multivolume. Sometimes, the best examinations of a topic come in a scholarly article or monograph exactly because its length limitations necessitate poignancy. So, in harkening to a generations-old practice, I offer this little bookling as a succinct (and yet hopefully substantial) study of an overlooked aspect of Abraham Lincoln's life.

LINCOLN THE INVENTOR

ABRAHAM LINCOLN'S
MECHANICAL MIND

Abraham Lincoln's invention and its subsequent patent always have been seen simply as a peculiar solitary event, a distraction from his politics, a historical footnote from the sideline of his life on his journey to greatness. Any books that mention the topic at all do so only perfunctorily. "The legend of Lincoln the prophet and martyr has bedimmed the genuine achievement of a human mind at work," Roy P. Basler once trenchantly wrote.[1] In truth, the story of Lincoln's invention—which was the physical fruition of an intensely curious and mechanical mind—is a significant milestone on his journey to immortality. The story runs much deeper and is more multifaceted than has been credited and offers another glimpse into the workings of Lincoln's much-examined intellect and character.

Benjamin P. Thomas once wrote, "Behind the solemn, furrowed countenance of Abraham Lincoln was an inquisitive mind. It ranged over the abstract and the infinite, the absolute and the immediate. It was philosophical, and at the same time intensely practical. On the practical level Lincoln's curiosity directed itself, among other things, to mechanical devices."[2] The story of Lincoln's invention involves not just a boat journey, the whittling of some wood, and a trip to the Patent Office; the invention had ramifications for Lincoln's life from the day his flatboat got stuck in 1831 till the day he died in 1865. It showed the mechanical genius of his mind and his way of thinking and analyzing, his penchant for expanding his learning and understanding disciplines other than politics, his fidelity to the political belief of internal improvements, his attempts at scholarly lecturing, and his admiration and fostering of invention and innovation as president. To understand Lincoln the inventor is to better understand Lincoln the man.

The story of Abraham Lincoln's invention of "a device to buoy vessels over shoals" began with a trip down the river. In April 1831, twenty-two-year-old Lincoln, his stepbrother, John D. Johnston, and his cousin John Hanks hired themselves out to merchant Denton Offutt to take a flatboat loaded with hogs and barrels of bacon, pork, and corn from Sangamo Town, Illinois, to the market at New Orleans.[3] Lincoln was an experienced boatman by this time (one reason he got the job), having worked plenty of jobs on the Ohio river, for the Portland Canal in Louisville, Kentucky, and Indiana, and as a hired hand on a flatboat to New Orleans in 1828.[4] During the 1831 trip, while descending the Sangamon River, Offutt's boat became grounded on the Rutledge milldam below the town of New Salem. With the front hanging out over the dam and the rear taking in water, Lincoln, wearing a pair of "mixed" blue jeans rolled up to his knees, "a hickory shirt and a Common Chip hat," began "straining every nerve" to pry the boat over the dam, stated witness William G. Greene.[5]

As the flatboat continued taking on water, Lincoln directed the crew to unload the hogs onto an adjacent boat. Lincoln ran into the village, borrowed an augur from the cooper shop, and bored a hole in the end of the boat hanging over the dam. Some of the cargo barrels were rolled to the bow, causing the boat to tilt, the water to drain out, and the boat to float free.[6] Every person in town showed up at the dam to watch the event, which lasted half a day and one night.[7] Impressed by Lincoln's operation on the dam, as well as his conduct during the entire journey to New Orleans, Offutt declared that he would build a steamboat for the Sangamon and have Lincoln as its captain. Offutt said he would build it with rollers underneath to overcome sandbars and runners underneath to run on ice, and "when Lincoln was captain by thunder she would have to go!"[8]

When his flatboat got stuck on the Rutledge milldam in New Salem, Illinois, in April 1831 and began taking on water, twenty-two-year-old Abraham Lincoln thought quickly and took charge. He directed the crew to unload the cargo as he ran into the village. With an augur borrowed from the cooper shop, he bored a hole in the end of the boat hanging over the dam and rolled some barrels to this hanging end, which allowed the water to drain out. He plugged the hole and guided the boat over the dam. Illustration by Lloyd Ostendorf, author of Abraham Lincoln: The Boy, The Man, reproduced courtesy of publisher Phil Wagner, Springfield, Illinois, www.abelincoln.com.

Offutt never built the steamboat, but he did open a general store in New Salem in August 1831 and hired Lincoln as a clerk. It was during his nearly six years at New Salem that Lincoln's self-reliant education took on a new, more expansive direction, and he honed his keen mind even sharper. Instead of being limited by few available books and little free time, as he was as a boy in Indiana, Lincoln made his own time to utilize numerous learning materials and to have educated men advise and mentor him.[9] Lincoln, with less than one year of formal schooling, read every book and newspaper he could acquire or borrow, taught himself the techniques of surveying, kept abreast of local and national political issues, and began his self-study of the law, which would become his profession.[10]

Seventeen years later, while Lincoln was a member of the U.S. House of Representatives, he and his family were traveling aboard the steamboat *Globe* over the Great Lakes from Buffalo, New York, to Chicago as they journeyed home to Springfield. Lincoln, the lone Whig Congressman from Illinois, had just finished giving political speeches across New England in support of General Zachary Taylor's 1848 presidential campaign.[11] As the *Globe* passed up the Detroit River during the final days of September, it came upon another steamboat, the *Canada*, which had run aground on Fighting Island.[12] From the deck of the *Globe*, Lincoln watched as the *Canada*'s captain ordered his crew to collect all the empty barrels, boxes, and loose planks on the ship and force them under the sides to buoy the boat over the shallow water.[13] No doubt this operation reminded Lincoln of his adventure at the New Salem milldam and got the old flat-boatman in him thinking of this common waterway problem. For the rest of his journey home, Lincoln considered how to construct a device to free stranded boats from shallow waters.

His idea was to use inflatable chambers—similar to giant bellows—attached on each side of the hull of a steamboat, or any other vessel, just below the water line. A system of sliding spars or shafts and ropes and pulleys filled the chambers with air. This inflation, achieved by either steam power or manpower, could be done whenever needed to buoy the ship over sandbars or other waterway obstructions and without discharging the ship's cargo.[14] In Lincoln's vision, the chambers could be inflated simultaneously or individually, as the case may require, and easily folded up for storage when not in use.[15] But Lincoln, true to his own indefatigable intellect and innovative spirit, was not content simply to think about a new invention. As Ralph Waldo Emerson said in 1837, for a true American scholar, "The preamble of thought, the transition through which it passes from the unconscious to the conscious, is action," for without action, "thought can never ripen into truth."[16] Lincoln's life was, by necessity, a life of action, and this experience he used and molded to attain his own achievements. In this instance, his years of experience as a boatman on the Sangamon, Illinois, and Mississippi rivers led him to his creation.

Abraham Lincoln and Springfield, Illinois, mechanic Walter Davis made this eighteen-inch model of Lincoln's invention of "a device to buoy vessels over shoals," which, in 1849, Lincoln submitted with his patent application to the U.S. Patent Office. Lincoln whittled the thicker interior frame posts with his pocketknife. The model currently is in the Smithsonian Institution. Photo courtesy National Museum of American History, Smithsonian Institution.

Lincoln spent the next eight weeks writing a description of his invention and making a model of his design.[17] Lincoln's law partner, William Herndon, remembered well his partner's work on his invention.

He was very much taken up with the project and, for a time, would slip away from the office and hurry down to the shop of Walter Davis, a Springfield mechanic, where, with the aid of the latter and the use of his tools, he gradually constructed the model and sent it to Washington. I often saw him tinkering in Davis's shop [one block west of the Lincoln & Herndon law office,] and, on one or two occasions, owing to his absence from the office, I had to go down there and confer with him regarding matters of business. When the model was done it was brought to the office, and, with the enthusiasm of the average inventor, Lincoln would expatiate on the marvels and merits of the device for the benefit of the few persons who dropped in and were sufficiently interested to listen to his vivid and rosy predictions.[18]

Lincoln also would work on the model in the office and, while whittling on it, talk about "the revolution it was destined to work" in steamboat navigation; "Although I regarded the thing as impracticable I said nothing, probably out of respect for Lincoln's well-known reputation as a boatman," Herndon said.[19]

Lincoln's ambition to build his "revolutionary" device was not as eccentric as it may sound, for Lincoln's mind was not solely preoccupied with law and politics. He had been a mechanically minded individual his entire life. His father, Thomas Lincoln, was, in fact, a carpenter and mechanic as well as a farmer; he built and repaired numerous structures and furniture pieces for his neighbors through the years, and he undoubtedly taught his son the trade.[20] Abraham Lincoln spent his years from ages four to twenty-one living the pioneer lifestyle in the intense manual labor of farming and assisting his father with carpentry. This life consisted of mechanical applications such as fixing farm machinery, understanding the architecture and using carpentry in building homes, and constructing and repairing outbuildings, barns, fences, furniture, and other necessary items. Abraham disliked such work, however, and would read books every chance he had. Neighbors thought young Lincoln was lazy for all the reading and thinking he did, to which he once responded that his father taught him to work but never taught him to love it.[21] His great dream as a child was to learn and to achieve success at something other than plowing fields. His years on the farm and in the wilderness, however, turned him into a skilled worker. Grant Goodrich, one of Lincoln's professional associates, later said Lincoln "had a great deal of Mechanical genius" and could understand easily why and how machines worked.[22]

Henry Clay Whitney, one of Lincoln's traveling companions on the Eighth Judicial Circuit, wrote of how, in the years before train travel, whenever the lawyers of the circuit would stop for dinner at a farmhouse, Lincoln would "improve the leisure" of the evening by "hunting up some farming implement, machine or tool" and begin probing.

> He would carefully examine it all over, first generally and then critically; he would "sight" it to determine if it was straight or warped: if he could make a practical test of it, he would do that; he would turn it over or around and stoop down, or lie down, if necessary, to look under it; he would examine it closely, then stand off and examine it at a little distance; he would shake it, lift it, roll it about, up-end it, overset it, and thus ascertain every quality and utility which inhered in it, so far as acute and patient investigation could do it. He was equally inquisitive in regard to matters which obtruded on his attention in the moral world; he would bore to the center of any moral proposition, and carefully analyze and dissect every layer and every atom of which it was composed, nor would he give over the search till completely satisfied that there was nothing more to know, or be learned about it.[23]

William Herndon also was a witness to his partner's mechanical mind. Lincoln would "stop in the street and analyze a machine. . . . [he would] whittle a thing to a point, and then count the numberless inclined planes and their pitch making the point. Mastering and defining this, he would then cut that point back and get a broad transverse section of his pine-stick, and peel and define that," Herndon stated. Clocks, omnibuses, language, paddle wheels, and idioms "never escaped his observation and analysis." Lincoln "threw his whole mental light around [an] object" when it was under his observation. "Not only were nature, man and principle suggestive to Mr. Lincoln, not only had he accurate and exact perceptions, but he was causative; his mind, apparently with an automatic movement, ran back behind facts, principles, and all things to their origin and first cause—to that point where forces act at once as effect and cause," Herndon related.[24]

Lincoln was so enamored of inventions and mechanics that during his first session as a Congressman, he took his four-year-old son, Robert, to the U.S. Patent Office to examine the invention models on public display.[25] The visit must have been an awe-inspiring revelation to the two Lincolns. The patent-office building, now the home of the Smithsonian's National Collection of Fine Arts, covers two city blocks and is an immense marble and columned structure, redolent of ancient Roman architecture.[26] The model room occupied the entire third floor of the building, consisted of four grand halls opening into each other, and contained about two hundred thousand models of American inventions as well as priceless items of historic interest and curiosity.[27] As one visitor described it, "For architectural simplicity and space, and the purpose for which it was designed, [the Model

The U.S. Patent Office Model Room, as it looked around 1870, held more than 200,000 models on display at that time. Abraham and Robert Lincoln looked through this room during Lincoln's first term as a U.S. Congressman, and Lincoln's own patent model resided here for a number of years during the 1850s. Illustration reprinted from Mary Clemmer Ames, *Ten Years in Washington: Life and Scenes in the National Capital, as a Woman Sees Them* (Hartford, CT: A. D. Worthington & Co., 1873).

Room] is unsurpassed in the whole world."[28] The models and other items on display were arranged in eight-by-eighteen-foot glass cases, placed so visitors could easily circumnavigate them and examine every side and angle of the contents. Models could be inspected anytime by anyone in the presence of a patent-office employee, and thousands of people yearly visited the gallery, according to one history of the patent office.[29] Lincoln and son, amazed at the number of inventions they saw there, decided that man's ingenuity and mastery over nature were so great, there was nothing new left to discover.[30]

William Herndon credited Lincoln's "failure" in Congress as "the beginning of an important epoch in his development. Believing he was politically moribund and yearning to broaden his knowledge, he turned most heartily to intensive study." This study had a decidedly scientific and mechanical penchant. Friends and colleagues of Lincoln testified to his study of mathematics, grammar, philosophy, science, and astronomy.[31] "I have seen him myself, upon the circuit, with 'a geometry,' or 'an astronomy,' or some book of that kind, working out propositions in moments of leisure," later recalled Leonard Swett, an attorney who also rode the Eighth Circuit with Lincoln.[32] Lincoln's journey toward education in fact began with "an old dog-eared arithmetic book" that his father determined his young son would "cipher clear through."[33] As a young man in New Salem, Lincoln supplemented his small income by working as an assistant to the surveyor of Sangamon County. Having no experience with the highly mathematical art of utilizing the square and compass, Lincoln taught himself the trade in six weeks by studying Abel Flint's *A System of Geometry and Trigonometry with a Treatise on Surveying* and Robert Gibson's *A Treatise on Practical Surveying*.[34] That Lincoln was of a mechanical mind needs little more proof than that he "nearly mastered" Euclid's geometry on his own during the late 1850s.[35] One 1867 newspaper article listed all the books on the Lincoln & Herndon law-office bookshelf, with titles such as *On the Correlation of Physical Forces* by Robert William Grove, *Elements of Punctuation* by John Wilson, *Elements of English Grammar* by Samuel Greene, *The Science of the Moral Nature* by George Giles Vincent, *The Skeptical Era in Modern History* by Truman M. Post, *A New Philosophy of Matter* by George Brewster, and Edward Hitchcock's *Elements of Zoology*.[36]

Herndon once related to his writing collaborator, Jesse Weik, how in 1858 he purchased the latest volume of *The Annual of Science*, to which Lincoln immediately took a great interest.[37] The purpose of the yearly periodical was to "record, teach, and fully explain" both the failures and successes of experiments of all philosophies and sciences. According to Herndon, upon perusing the opening pages of the book, Lincoln immediately left the office and bought all the previous issues back to its first printing in 1850. "I have wanted such a book for years," Lincoln reportedly said, "because I sometimes make experiments and have thoughts about the physical world that I do not know to be true or false. I may, by this book, correct my errors and save time and expense."[38]

One such example of Lincoln's scientific thoughts involved the problems of constructing an agricultural steam plow that would put more power into plowing a field than into its actual propulsion. "I have thought a good deal, in an abstract way, about a Steam Plow," he told the Wisconsin State Agricultural Society in a September 1859 address. And although he had not discovered the solution to the problem, he was sure that smarter men than he would, if they had not already, find it. Lincoln's Wisconsin address was overall a consideration of free labor principles versus slave labor principles and how "Free Labor insists on universal education." The educated laborer then, while seeking to improve the product of his labor, will become innovative. Such discovery and invention were essential to the farmer in his productivity. "No other human occupation opens so wide a field for the profitable and agreeable combination of labor with cultivated thought, as agriculture," Lincoln declared. "I know of nothing so pleasant to the mind, as the discovery of anything which is at once new and valuable—nothing which so lightens and sweetens toil, as the hopeful pursuit of such discovery. And how vast, and how varied a field is agriculture, for such discovery."[39] Lincoln's address also revealed perhaps the inception of his own examinations and interest of such mechanical improvements, while himself growing to manhood on a pioneer farmstead.

The mind, already trained to thought, in the country school, or higher school, cannot fail to find there [in agriculture] an exhaustless source of profitable enjoyment. Every blade of grass is a study; and to produce two, where there was but one, is both a profit and a pleasure. And not grass alone; but soils, seeds, and seasons—hedges, ditches, and fences, draining, droughts, and irrigation—plowing, hoeing, and harrowing—reaping, mowing, and threshing—saving crops, pests of crops, diseases of crops, and what will prevent or cure them—implements, utensils, and machines, their relative merits, and [how] to improve them—hogs, horses, and cattle—sheep, goats, and poultry—trees, shrubs, fruits, plants, and flowers—the thousand things of which these are specimens—each a world of study within itself.[40]

Like the innovations of the educated agriculturalist, Lincoln's steamboat invention was utilitarian and not simply an exercise of his intellect or a self-aggrandizing means of fame and fortune (although if his model had been manufactured and he had realized some profit, he surely would not have complained or refused). Growing up as a pioneer farmer and boatman, Lincoln knew the necessity for reliable transportation not just for travel but also to take farm products to market, and he hoped his invention would help facilitate river navigation. It was the realization of Lincoln's understanding of the needs of the western American as well as an outgrowth of his long-held political belief in internal improvements. Lincoln had championed Henry Clay's American System since his first term as a state legislator in 1834 and continued it into his presidential terms.

Even in his first failed run for state legislator in 1832, Lincoln focused his campaign on his great belief in the creation of good roads, bridges, railways, and canals and the clearing of impediments to improve river travel. "Time and experience have verified to a demonstration, the public utility of internal improvements," Lincoln declared, "That the poorest and most thinly populated countries would be greatly benefited by the opening of good roads, and in the clearing of navigable streams within their limits, is what no person will deny." He also mentioned his own experience as a flat-boatman, and even of getting stuck on the Rutledge milldam, as proof of his knowledge of the subject.[41]

Throughout his ensuing four terms in the Illinois state legislature, from 1834 to 1842, Lincoln was a vociferous supporter of internal improvements and achieved much advancement and development for Sangamon County and the entire state. He once said that "his highest ambition was to become the DeWitt Clinton of Illinois," according to his friend Joshua Speed.[42] As a member of the U.S. House of Representatives from 1847 to 1849, Lincoln continued to advocate internal improvements and even gave a speech on the House floor solely dedicated to it.[43] As president, Lincoln continually espoused the importance of building and improving the American transportation infrastructure—and, concomitantly, westward expansion and agricultural improvements—in his annual messages to Congress.[44]

The great discussion for improved transportation in Springfield and vicinity from 1847 to 1849 in fact led Lincoln, after eight weeks of thought and dedicated work on his invention, to exhibit his device to curious townspeople as proof of his belief that steamboat navigation on and from the Sangamon River through the Illinois River and into the Mississippi River, was practicable. At two o'clock on a November day in 1848, Lincoln brought the recently completed model of his invention to buoy vessels over shoals to "the big water trough at the corner opposite" from his office.[45] As witness Gaius Paddock later related:

> Quite a crowd had gathered as the word had been passed around the streets. He appeared with his four foot model under his arm and approaching the trough, which had been pumped full and announced "now is the time to witness the successful navigation by 'model of the Sangamon' and other rivers that have bars and shoal places." He then proceeded to put his model boat afloat in the water and placing a few bricks upon it until it sank to the first deck, he then applied the air pumps modeled like the old fire bellows, four in number, two on each side that were beneath the lower or first deck and in a few moments it slowly

In November 1848, Abraham Lincoln demonstrated his patent model in a horse trough near his law office to a group of onlookers. One witness later wrote, "The crowd listened to Lincoln's defense of his invention, gave three cheers and dispersed, much impressed but not fully convinced." Illustration by Lloyd Ostendorf, author of *Abraham Lincoln: The Boy, the Man*, reproduced courtesy of publisher Phil Wagner, Springfield, Illinois, www.abelincoln.com.

rose above the water about six inches, Lincoln remarking that each inch represented a foot, on a good sized steam boat. This novel invention surely demonstrated it was possible to have water communication on the Sangamon. There were yet some doubters, as to its practicability for actual transportation. The crowd listened to Lincoln's defense of his invention, gave three cheers and dispersed, much impressed but not fully convinced. He retired with his model under his arm, remarking if they had any more questions to ask, they could do so and answer them or not, as he had no further information to give.[46]

When Lincoln left Springfield to return to Washington in late November 1848 for the next Congressional session, he took his model with him. Lincoln hired attorney Zenas C. Robbins to assist him in obtaining a patent. Robbins later recalled Lincoln's 1848 visit to his office.

He walked into my office one morning with a model of a western steamboat under his arm. After a friendly greeting he placed his model on my office-table and proceeded to explain the principles embodied therein that he believed to be his own invention, and which, if new, he desired to secure by letters-patent. During my former residence in St. Louis, I had made myself thoroughly familiar with everything appertaining to the construction and equipment of the flat-bottomed steamboats that were adapted to the shallow rivers of our western and southern States, and therefore, I was able speedily to come to the conclusion that Mr. Lincoln's proposed improvement of that class of vessels was new and patentable, and I so informed him. Thereupon he instructed me to prepare the necessary drawings and papers and prosecute an application for a patent for his invention at the United State patent office.[47]

Legend states that Whig Senator Daniel Webster—by 1849 a giant in American politics—assisted Lincoln in obtaining his patent. According to tradition, Webster and Lincoln agreed on all the major issues of the day, and Webster held the lone Illinois Whig in higher esteem than other new congressmen; another tradition is that Lincoln often was a guest at Webster's famous Saturday-morning stag breakfasts.[48] This tradition then bolsters the imputation from a cryptic February 28, 1849 letter in which Webster informed Lincoln, "Mr. Ewbank is yet in doubt. If the enclosed statement of claim will satisfy our friends, I have reason to think a Patent may be obtained."[49] Unfortunately, the enclosure is unknown. While the date seems plausible to conclude that the letter referred to Lincoln's patent—which more than one historian has done—there is no verifiable proof.[50] However, as suggested by historian Wayne C. Temple, Lincoln knew that political support always expedited business in Washington, and, knowing this, it is logical to assume that he asked the famous Webster for assistance.[51]

Lincoln submitted his patent application for a device for "Buoying Vessels over Shoals," along with his model, to the U.S. Patent Office on March 10, 1849, at which time he personally appeared, swore an oath to its originality before a Washington justice of the peace, and paid a thirty-dollar fee.[52] In April, Robbins informed Lincoln the patent was approved and would be issued one month later.[53] The patent was approved as Patent Number 6,469 on May 22, 1849.[54]

It appears that after all his work, Lincoln did nothing to publicize or market his invention. His collected writings, in fact, show no evidence that he ever thought about it again. As patent-office historian Harry Goldsmith states, the creation "just became another one among those thousands of patents which fail of commercial success."[55] William Herndon more simply, and somewhat more harshly, called it, "a perfect failure."[56] Gaius Paddock, the store clerk who heard Lincoln espouse his invention and then witnessed its exhibition, later said he felt Lincoln never attempted to market his device or invent any others because his "master mind" was "filled with intense thoughts of more grave importance."[57] Historian Mark E. Neely suggested Lincoln's invention went nowhere "probably because the weight of the apparatus would cause the problem he was trying to solve," that is, grounding the boat in the river bottom.[58] Whatever the explanation, more than one historian has surmised that Lincoln's invention may have furthered modern technology more than critics realize and that the engineering ideas behind his buoyant chambers actually may have advanced the creation of modern ship salvaging and submarine construction.[59]

Despite the denouement of his own patent, Lincoln's admiration and wonder for discoveries and inventions never abated. While a Congressman, Lincoln assisted at least two of his constituents with applying for their own patents.[60] As a lawyer, Lincoln took on at least five patent cases. His first was that of *Parker v. Hoyt*, an 1850 suit concerning patent infringement of a water wheel, in which Lincoln was one of the counsel for the defense.[61] His associate on the case, Grant Goodrich, later recollected that Lincoln took "great interest" in the case. "He had tended a saw-mill for some time, and was able in his arguments to explain the action of the water upon the wheel, in a manner so clear and intelligible, that the jury was enabled to comprehend the points and the line of defense. It was evident he had carried the jury with him, in a most masterly argument, the force of which could not be broken by the reply of opposing counsel."[62] Lincoln won the suit, a result that he "always regarded as one of the most gratifying triumphs of his life," Goodrich stated.[63]

One of the cases of the most interest to Lincoln appears to have been the 1855 "Horological Cradle" case of *Hildreth v. Turner*, involving the patent on an automatic cradle-rocking machine.[64] The cradle, being wound up and using a system of weights and pulleys, would rock itself and save the mother continual labor. The inventor, Alexander Edmonds, had sold the manufacture and sale rights for five states to William Turner for $10,000. Turner then sold part of his rights to others, who failed to repay their promissory notes. Turner sued, and the defendants hired Lincoln and Herndon. Lincoln, "owing to his natural bent for the study of mechanical appliances," was "so enamoured of the case" that he took complete charge of it, according to Herndon. For a time, the cradle was exhibited in a store window in Springfield and eventually in the Lincoln-Herndon law office, where Lincoln would "dilate at great length on its merits" to all callers. During the trial, the device was brought into court where Lincoln likewise enlightened the judges on its construction and use.[65] The legal argument turned on whether or not Edmonds actually had a patent on his cradle and the mechanisms and mode of its operation or simply for the cradle's ornamental design. Lincoln and Herndon argued that the patent was for the cradle, not the design. The Illinois Supreme Court disagreed.

In 1858, Lincoln worked a similar case with a similar courtroom exposition showing his grasp and fascination with mechanical devices. In *Rugg v. Haines*, Lincoln represented a man (Haines) suing another (Rugg) for patent infringement on a reaping machine; Rugg responded by accusing Haines of stealing his idea from an earlier model by a man named Esterly.[66] During the trial, all three models of reapers were brought into the courtroom where Lincoln explained their similarities and differences to the jury. Robert R. Hitt, who recorded the testimony for one of the attorneys (and later reported the Lincoln-Douglas debates for the *Chicago Tribune*), wrote in his journal, "To one unaccustomed to such things, the models of both the litigants' machines seemed to vary scarcely at all from each other but before the trial was over no juryman was so dull as not to have seen the light but important points of difference in each from the others, the qualities common to all, for three machines figured in the case."[67]

Charles S. Zane, William Herndon's law partner after Lincoln assumed the presidency, also recollected Lincoln's "faculty for comprehending and understanding machinery" during a patent-case argument he personally witnessed that was most likely *Rugg v. Haines*, although Zane did not specify the case. He recollected that numerous models representing different machines were introduced as evidence at trial, and, as Lincoln expounded on the machines, a number of jurors knelt down with him to get a better view, at which one of the opposing counsel purportedly said, "I guess our case has gone to h—l; Lincoln and the jurors are on their knees together."[68]

Lincoln's most famous patent suit was the 1856 "Reaper Case," *McCormick v. Manny et al.*, in which Cyrus McCormick, inventor of the revolutionary reaping machine, sued a rival manufacturer, John H. Manny, for patent infringement. The defense retained renowned patent attorney George Harding, who in turn brought on Lincoln as a well-known local lawyer to assist at the Chicago trial.[69] Harding, however, asked well-known attorney Edwin M. Stanton to assist as he found Lincoln an uncouth, inexperienced rube. Lincoln was not told of the change and prepared for the case more than he had ever prepared for any other, seeing possible fame in winning such a monumental argument. Part of his preparation included going to Manny's reaper factory outside Chicago and spending "half a day, examining and studying" Manny's machine.[70]

When he arrived at Cincinnati, the new location of the trial, Harding and Stanton insulted, humiliated; and disregarded Lincoln and ordered him to excuse himself from the case. Lincoln stayed the week in Cincinnati, however, and watched the entire trial, which his side won. On his return to Springfield, he was reluctant to talk about the experience, other than that he had been "roughly handled" by Harding and Stanton.[71] The episode, however, greatly influenced Lincoln's life. As his legal colleague Ralph Emerson said, Lincoln's command of language and courtroom style utilizing pertinent stories to illustrate his points were effective in Illinois, but "some of these stories were such as a gentleman of refinement would neither tell nor wish to hear." After watching the trial and seeing how polished, elaborate, and thoroughly prepared were the eastern lawyers on both sides of the case, Lincoln realized his own deficiencies and declared, "I am going home to study law." Emerson replied, "That is what you have been doing." "No," Lincoln said, "not as these college bred men study it. I have learned my lesson. These college bred fellows have reached Ohio, they will soon be in Illinois, and when they come . . . I will be ready for them."[72]

Lincoln's final patent case—in fact the final case prior to his election to the presidency—was *Dawson v. Ennis*, an infringement case argued in June 1860 while Lincoln was the Republican candidate for president. Lincoln represented the plaintiff in his suit for $10,000, alleging that Ennis had sold an improved patented double plow he had agreed not to sell.[73] The decision for the defendant was handed down five days after Lincoln's inauguration as president.

Lincoln's interest in patents and inventions was so deep that after his 1858 loss to Stephen A. Douglas for the Illinois U.S. Senate seat, Lincoln finalized a lecture on "Discoveries and Inventions," which he delivered six times between April 1858 and April 1860.[74] William

Abraham Lincoln sits for a portrait in the late 1850s, around the time he was delivering his "Lecture on Discoveries and Inventions" throughout Illinois. The self-assurance and determination in his face were not atypical, and they are certainly traits necessary to all inventors. As presidential secretary John Hay later wrote, "It is absurd to call [Lincoln] a modest man. No great man was ever modest. It was his intellectual arrogance but unconscious assumption of superiority that men like [Salmon P.] Chase and [Charles] Sumner never could forgive." Photo courtesy Library of Congress.

Herndon claimed the lecture sprung from Lincoln's need for sup-plemental income after the high expense of his senate campaign.[75] Whether Lincoln wrote it for money is not clear, but this lecture was undeniably the culmination of years of Lincoln's thought on a subject about which he was passionate. Henry Clay Whitney, in fact, recalled that Lincoln told him in 1855 that the lecture was something he had been contemplating "for some time."[76] Lincoln later synopsized the lecture as examining the origin of inventions and showing there is nothing new to be invented; that "all the modern inventions were known centuries ago."[77]

"All creation is a mine, and every man, a miner," opened Lincoln's lecture. "Man is not the only animal who labors; but he is the only one who *improves* his workmanship. This improvement, he effects by *Discoveries* and *Inventions*."[78] Lincoln began by briefly charting the history of human invention, which, he stated, commenced with the invention of the fig-leaf apron. Being clothed then gave man the freedom to continue to improve himself with inventions of iron tools, transportation, and agricultural devices.[79] "In the world's his-tory, certain inventions and discoveries occurred, of peculiar value, on account of their great efficiency in facilitating other inventions and discoveries," Lincoln said. In addition to the fig-leaf apron, the great inventions in Lincoln's opinion were the arts of writing and printing, the discovery of America, and the introduction of patent laws.[80]

These inventions followed in a logical line of world progress. The art of writing—which "to *it* we owe everything which distinguishes us from savages"—gave man the chances of invention, discovery and improvement by allowing the innovations of one person to be known and augmented upon by future generations. The invention of printing allowed writing to disseminate across the world to all peoples, but it was "a habit of freedom of thought" that allowed discoveries and inventions and improvements to take root. This habit was established and spread through the discovery of America and the influence of its free and open society on the rest of the world. This was the mean-ing of one of Lincoln's earlier points of the triumph and superior-ity of Young America versus Old Fogyism: "In anciently inhabited countries, the dust of ages—a real downright old-fogyism—seems to settle upon, and smother the intellects and energies of man," he said.

But the great fostering of innovation in America came with the adoption of patent laws in the Constitution.[81] "Before then, any man might instantly use what another had invented; so that the inventor had no special advantage from his own invention. The patent system changed this; secured to the inventor, for a limited time, the exclusive use of his invention; and thereby added the fuel of *interest* to the *fire* of genius, in the discovery and production of new and useful things," Lincoln said.[82] This last clause of Lincoln's lecture has come to be one of his more famous aphorisms, and its paraphrase, in fact, is etched in marble above the northeast entrance of the U.S. Patent Office.

Lincoln's lecture was the culmination of years of thought; it was not idle speculation or fanciful rhetoric. Lincoln had actually succeeded in accomplishing what he spoke of—the greatness of ambition and evolution—with the patent of his own invention in 1849 and then again with the publication and copyright of his debates with Stephen A. Douglas in 1859. Here Lincoln had achieved exactly what he believed to be the quintessence of man's greatness and advancement and determination: he had created an actual mechanical device to help improve man's labor and increase his bounty and life enjoyment and had created a document of words and ideas that, by being published and copyrighted, could inspire others through its ideas, while its originality and perpetuity were guarded by copyright protection. Lincoln, here, actually practiced what he preached and encouraged others to do the same.

Lincoln was, of course, a political man and a man of great intellect. It should be no surprise, therefore, that his theme of the benefits of discoveries and inventions segued into his speech before the Wisconsin agricultural fair in 1859 about technological advance and free-labor principles. The agricultural life, he believed, engendered individual responsibility and tempered the hunger of rich men for mediocre farming of huge tracts of land. What Lincoln alluded to here was that such immense landowners, of course, utilized slaves. Concomitantly, improvements in technology, Lincoln believed, would foster economic development, which would in turn make slavery unnecessary and untenable. This idea that slavery is not only inhuman to the slaves but also suffocating of intellect and vitality to the master is one of which Lincoln had spoken often. In fact, he continued his logical demolition of the arguments in favor of slavery just a few months later in his Cooper Union address in New York City in 1860.

At the time of its delivery, however, Lincoln's lecture on discoveries and inventions seems not to have been so highly regarded. While the newspapers in Jacksonville and Springfield, Illinois, called it "highly entertaining" and "received with repeated and hearty bursts of applause" and encouraged attendance of future dates for what "we are assured will be an 'intellectual feast,'" specific attendees were not so generous.[83] William Herndon—albeit writing more than thirty years after the speech was delivered—judged it to be "a cold flat thing."

> I know that Mr. L was not fitted, qualified, in any way to deliver a lecture to our people, who were intelligent, well read, and well educated. I was not mistaken in the lecture which Mr. L read; it was a lifeless thing, a dull dead thing, "died aborning." It fell on the ears of the audience. . . . There was no life, imagination, or fancy in it, no spirit and no life. The whole thing was a kind of farce and injured Mr. L's reputation as a man of sense among his friends and enemies.[84]

William Jayne, a member of Phi Alpha, said the audience in Jacksonville was small, and receipts at the door were "proportionately disappointing, a fact that Mr. Lincoln could not fail to note."[85] College student J. H. Burnham paid twenty-five cents to hear Lincoln speak in Bloomington, Illinois, but the crowd was so small—only about forty people—that "Old Abe would not speak to such a small crowd, and they paid us back our quarters at the door."[86] This was an embarrassing event for Lincoln, so much so that when his friend Henry Clay Whitney teased him about it later, Lincoln responded, "Don't mention that, for it plagues me some."[87] One attendee at Lincoln's lecture in Pontiac, Illinois, gave a similar review, saying Lincoln "is a 'Big Gun' in the political world but—I think the people generally were disappointed in his lecture as it was on no particular subject and not well connected. He was, I thought, decidedly inferior to many a lecturer I have seen."[88] Lincoln later refused invitations to deliver his lecture in Galesburg and Rock Island, Illinois, citing the pressure of legal business.[89] Herndon later said, "Mr. Lincoln was Lawyer, Politician, Lecturer, and Inventor. He succeeded in the law and politics, was an utter failure as lecturer and inventor."[90] Lincoln may or may not have agreed with his partner's assessment of his lecturing skills. He did once refer to his first attempt at a lecture as "rather a poor one;" but upon being encouraged to finish the lecture in January 1865 by Harvard professor Louis Agassiz, Lincoln said he had the manuscript somewhere in his papers, and "When I get out of this place, I'll finish it up, perhaps, and get my friend [journalist Noah Brooks] to print it somewhere."[91]

After Lincoln's election to the presidency, his unique stature as the only president to hold a patent did not go unnoticed. The weekly *Scientific American* ran an illustrated article about Lincoln's invention, describing it in detail. While the editors stated the invention "illustrates forcibly the variety of talents possessed by men," they also offered a none-too-subtle jab at its merits: "We hope the author of it will have better success in presiding as Chief Magistrate over the people of the entire Union than he has had as an inventor in introducing his invention upon the western waters, for which it was specially designed."[92]

Lincoln's patent may have been rediscovered, but his model had long been relegated to obscurity on the shelves of the Patent Office.[93] Shortly after his inauguration, Lincoln directed a patent-office employee to find his model for him.[94] In April 1861, *Harper's Weekly* also commented on Lincoln's patent.

> Among the registered patents in the Patent Office at Washington is one for buoying vessels through shallow waters, taken out some years ago by Abraham Lincoln, of Springfield, Illinois. The method is by the employment of air-chambers constructed on the principle of a bellows, and distended or contracted by ropes, as the depth of water may require. It was by a somewhat similar scheme, on a larger scale, that it was once proposed to

bring the Great Eastern through the East River to a dock. The inventor, Mr. Lincoln, has not had the satisfaction of seeing his patent in use on the Mississippi or its tributaries.

But it has fallen to his lot to be in command of a ship of uncommon burden on a voyage of uncommon danger. It devolves upon him to navigate the ship of state through shallows of unprecedented peril, and over flats of unparalleled extent. The difficulty is how to prevent her grounding and becoming a wreck.

We trust that the President will set the fashion of using his own patent.

He must throw some of his cargo overboard, and buoy up his craft on all sides. He need not change his voyage, or sail for a strange port. But unless he can set his air-chambers at work so as to diminish the draught of his vessel—in a word, unless he can increase her buoyancy, and bring more of her hull into God's daylight, he will run no small risk of losing her altogether.[95]

History has shown that Lincoln did indeed use his multifaceted intellect and his abiding belief in innovation to progress the Union cause during the war. As president, Lincoln fostered invention—and even signed a bill creating the National Academy of Sciences in 1863—and always was eager and willing to hear new ideas by inventors.[96] As the *Scientific American* editorialized just after the beginning of the war, "Times of war have generally been times of great mental activity; fruitful in novel ideas and inventions. . . . The great war which has been inaugurated in our midst will doubtless produce many wonderful developments, and it will be very interesting to observe, whether, among these, will be a greater degree of activity on the part of inventors even than that which has marked our past periods of peace."[97]

Indeed, immediately upon the attack on Fort Sumter, inventors flocked to the White House to offer Lincoln their ideas for improvements in military hardware. "The inventors were more a source of amusement than annoyance," wrote Lincoln's secretary

John Hay. "They were usually men of some originality of character, not infrequently carried to eccentricity."[98] But, in accordance with his mechanical mind, Lincoln was much interested in their offerings.

> Lincoln had a quick comprehension of mechanical principles, and often detected a flaw in an invention which the contriver had overlooked. He would sometimes go out to the waste fields that then lay south of the Executive mansion to test an experimental gun or torpedo. . . . He was particularly interested in the first rude attempts at the afterwards famous mitrailleuses; on one occasion he worked one with his own hands at the Arsenal, and sent forth peals of Homeric laughter as the balls, which had not power to penetrate the target set up at a little distance, came bounding back among the shins of the bystanders. He accompanied Colonel Hiram Berdan one day to the camp of his sharpshooters and there practiced in the trenches his long disused skill with the rifle.[99]

Lincoln's encouragement of invention from 1861 to 1865 was so vast, in fact, as to be the subject of an entire book, *Lincoln and the Tools of War*, by Robert V. Bruce. Among the myriad creations fostered and utilized by the Union during the war, Lincoln encouraged such items as machine guns, breach-loading guns, breach-loading cannons, rockets, projectiles, explosives, flamethrowers, the observation balloon, submarines, naval armor, new gunpowders, a floating harbor obstruction, and new ways to protect wooden structures from fire.[100] He even had his own idea to create a steam ram for use as harbor defenses, "as a Bull-dog guards his master's door."[101]

Lincoln also took great enjoyment in going to the Washington Navy Yard, home of naval ordnance, to examine, witness, and test new firearms. He often consulted Navy Yard Captain John A. Dahlgren on new inventions and weapons, and the two men quickly became warm friends.[102] One incident between them illustrates not only their friendship and working relationship but also Lincoln's scientific inquisitiveness. In December 1862, Dahlgren visited Lincoln in the White House. After discussing the "troublesome business" of the war, Lincoln relaxing into his usual humor, sat down and said, "Well, Captain, here's a letter about a new powder," which he read, and showed the sample. Said he had burned some, and there was too much residuum. "Now, I'll show you." So he got a small sheet of paper, placed it on some of the powder, ran to the fire, and with tongs picked up a coal, which he blew, specks still on his nose. It occurred to me how peaceful was his mind, so easily diverted from the great convulsion going on, and a nation menaced with disruption.

The president clapped the coal to the powder and away it went, he remarking, "There is too much left there." He handed me a small parcel of the powder to try.[103]

Lincoln visited the Navy Yard practically every week for the first two years of the war.[104] While Lincoln's visits certainly were the product of his inquisitive mind coupled with his pragmatic needs as commander-in-chief, they were also times of refuge, relaxation, and refreshment for the beleaguered president.[105] Dahlgren's diaries show that many of Lincoln's visits began as discussions about ordnance or new inventions and continued as social visits.

To posterity, Lincoln's fostering of innovation appears logical and practical, but to officials at the Navy Department, Lincoln's activities in this regard were troublesome. Upon hearing that Lincoln had given written promise to a man named Dillon for $150,000 if a newly invented gunpowder should prove effective, Navy Secretary Gideon Welles called Lincoln's penchant for encouraging invention "well-intentioned but irregular" and worried that "the president, who has a propensity to engage in matters of this kind . . . is liable to be constantly imposed upon by sharpers and adventurers. Finding the heads of departments opposed to these schemes, the president goes often behind them, as in this instance; and subordinates, flattered by his notice, encourage him."[106] Dahlgren, who admired Lincoln greatly, nevertheless also once called it "unfortunate" that the president would "meddle" in such matters as securing military contracts.[107]

After Lincoln's death, the patent model for his invention to buoy vessels over shoals was placed for display in the U.S. Patent Office model room. A reporter from the *Boston Daily Advertiser* went to the patent office in May 1865 to see "the little model which, in ages to come, will be prized as at once one of the most curious and one of the most sacred relics in that vast museum of unique and priceless things."[108] His description, mingled with the post-assassination reverence for a martyr, is the only known contemporary and nonscientific description of the model.

> The model, which is about eighteen or twenty inches long, and has the air of having been whittled with a knife out of a shingle and a cigar box, is built without any elaboration or ornament, or any extra apparatus beyond the necessary to show the operation of buoying the steamer over the obstructions. Herein it differs from very many of the models which share with it the shelter of the immense halls of the Patent Office, and which are fashioned with wonderful nicety and exquisite finish, as if much of the labor and thought and affection of a lifetime had been devoted to their construction. This is a model of a different kind; carved as one might imagine a retired rail-splitter would whittle, strongly but not smoothly, and evidently made with a view solely to convey, by the simplest possible means, to the minds of the patent authorities, an idea of the purpose and plan of the simple invention.[109]

The editors of the *Scientific American*, returning upon their 1860 article about Lincoln's invention, gave succinct paean in 1865 to the dead president and, instead of their previous subtle criticism, used the inevitable metaphor to praise Lincoln's "skill in buoying the great vessel of state over dangerous breakers" that has "made his name honored throughout the whole civilized world."[110]

Not long after Lincoln's death, a second model of his invention was discovered by his brother-in-law Clark Moulton Smith in the attic of Lincoln's Springfield home, and given to Shurtleff College, in Alton, Illinois.[111] The college closed in 1957, the buildings and their contents acquired by Southern Illinois University. The location of Lincoln's second, personal model is unknown.[112]

Abraham Lincoln as inventor is a story generally known but rarely examined to reveal its larger meaning. Lincoln's mechanical mind gave America more than just an unmanufactured invention; it was more than just the momentary élan or peculiarity of an intellectual man. The depth of Lincoln's scientific thinking—brought to fruition with his invention—pervaded his entire life and contributed to his overall greatness. His desire for cultural and social advancement and improvement through innovation influenced his thinking on internal improvements, free labor and slavery, and the tools of war; his penchant for math and science reflected his desire for exactness in everything he did, from surveying, to the law, to military planning, and even to his study of grammar and his writing. As acclaimed intellectual Jacques Barzun declared, Lincoln's "artistic genius"—as poet, writer, inventor, scholar, orator, and politician—was the reason he was a man able to "master a dangerous, new, and sophisticated world."[113]

While Lincoln occupies the unique place in American history as the only president to hold a patent, he also created numerous other inventions during his life, not of wood but of words. Lincoln's printed speeches and writings—no less inventions for not being of tangible physical matter—arguably have had the greatest impact of all his works since his death. "He is a creative consciousness in whom the enduring matter of Civil War America lives," Roy P. Basler declares. "As this subject matter is in Lincoln intrinsic and his expression of it inimitable so his works will endure, as something representative and symbolic, with singular completeness of the epoch which nurtured him."[114] As Lincoln himself said in his lecture on discoveries and inventions, "In one word, by means of *writing*, the seeds of invention were more permanently preserved, and more widely sown."[115]

Lincoln's patent model today survives in the Smithsonian Institution's National Museum of American History in Washington, D.C., while the words of his lecture on "Discoveries and Inventions" also live within the nation's capital, etched in marble above the entrance to the U.S. Patent Office.[116] Likewise, the words of his "House Divided" speech, Gettysburg Address, and Second Inaugural Address, to name but a few, also redound through history and have inspired countless generations. In this way, the tangible and intangible aspects of Lincoln's creations swell and blend together in a great chorus of invention. The inquisitiveness of his mind, the mechanical bent of his interests, molded him into the student, lawyer, inventor, politician, and citizen that he was. This was his genius: his indefatigable desire to advance his knowledge, to create, and to improve the world in which he lived by that creation.

LINCOLN'S LECTURE ON
DISCOVERIES AND INVENTIONS:
THE UNKNOWN DRAFT

A braham Lincoln's lecture on discoveries and inventions is an important and interesting parenthesis on his road to the presidency. It occurred between his loss to Stephen A. Douglas for the 1858 Illinois U.S. Senate seat and his 1860 election to the presidency. The lecture offers evidence of the depth and breadth of Lincoln's wonderful mental capabilities and shows that although today he is a secular godhead, not every action he undertook during his life was free from self-interest, or even from nominal failure. And when considered amid Lincoln's other great writings and speeches—the Gettysburg Address, the Second Inaugural Address, the Emancipation Proclamation—it fails to excite much interest or examination.

The history of the physical aspect of the lecture—the pieces of paper on which it was written—has long been known, but it also has been studied, since the papers that exist are in no way a final draft. In fact, the dissembled pieces of paper that for years were considered two lectures have been proven in recent years to be different sections of the same one. But still, the papers that now reside in the Lincoln collections of a Japanese and an Illinois university are not complete. Believing that Abraham Lincoln, with his meticulous nature and adherence to accuracy, as well as his typical avoidance of extemporaneous speaking during the late 1850s and into the 1860s, would not have given the same lecture six times without having completed it and written it down in a finalized form, the questions must be asked, Was there ever a "final" draft? If so, what happened to it?

A survey of correspondence between Robert T. Lincoln, one of the president's sons and the only one to live into adulthood, and John G. Nicolay, the president's private secretary, has revealed new and previously unpublished facts about an unknown version of the lecture, how Robert lost it and tried to find it, the indifference with which Robert and Nicolay held the lecture, and their decision to give it as little attention as possible when publishing President Lincoln's collected works.

Abraham Lincoln's lecture on discoveries and inventions began as an idea perhaps as early as 1849, after the completion of his single term in Congress and the patent of his original invention of a device to buoy vessels over shoals. Although the lecture's inception is unknown for certain, Nicolay—who relied heavily upon Robert

John G. Nicolay (*left*) and Robert T. Lincoln (*right*) were friends from the 1860s until Nicolay's death in 1901. Nicolay, along with John Hay, wrote a ten-volume biography of Abraham Lincoln and edited a two-volume collected works, all at Robert's behest and with his assistance. John Nicolay photo courtesy Library of Congress; Robert Lincoln photo courtesy Hildene, The Lincoln Family Home, Manchester, Vermont.

Lincoln's memory and advice—surmised that it must have been written "at odd moments" between 1849 and its first delivery in 1858.[1] Lincoln's law partner, William Herndon, recalled Lincoln preparing the lecture in 1858 "in his usual way by noting down ideas on stray pieces of paper, which found a lodgment inside his hat."[2] What is known, however, is that while riding the Eighth Judicial Circuit in 1855, Lincoln told his colleagues Henry Clay Whitney and Leonard Swett that he long had been contemplating the writing of a lecture on man; "he said he proposed to review man from his earliest primeval state to his present high development, and he detailed at length the views and opinions he designed to incorporate into his lecture," Whitney recalled.[3]

Lincoln's expatiation on the topic resulted from the three men, while riding the circuit between Urbana and Danville, Illinois, reading from historian George Bancroft's 1854 lecture on the progress of man.[4] The three lawyers read aloud by turns, "stopping frequently to comment upon the text at the appropriate places."[5] Bancroft had declared that the previous fifty years were a time of unequaled discoveries and deeds by man, accomplished with the divine assistance of God. Lincoln admitted his idea to be somewhat similar. "His purpose," Whitney wrote, "was to analyze inventions and discoveries— 'to get at the bottom of things'; and to show when, where, how, and why such things were invented or discovered; and, so far as possible, to find where the first mention is made of some of the common things. The Bible, he said, he found to be the richest store-house for such knowledge."[6] As president, Lincoln synopsized his lecture by saying, "I think I can show, at least in a fanciful way, that all modern inventions were known centuries ago."[7]

Lincoln's interest in the lecture circuit did not begin with his thoughts on discoveries and inventions. In 1838, he spoke in Springfield to the Young Men's Lyceum on "The Perpetuation of Our Political Institutions"; in 1842, he spoke to the Springfield Washington Temperance Society; and in the early 1850s, he gave eulogies on Zachary Taylor and Henry Clay.[8] After delivering his lecture on discoveries and inventions numerous times, Lincoln also spoke on labor and democracy at the Wisconsin State Agricultural Fair.[9] He began—but never completed—notes in 1848 for lectures at Niagara Falls and in the early 1850s on the practice of law.[10] Lecturing was common in the mid-nineteenth century. American lyceums were popular attractions designed to educate, enrich, and inspire people in an age when reading, discourse and attending such intellectual events were as common as watching television is today.[11]

Lincoln's lecture on discoveries and inventions was not a passing whim or a half-hearted composition. It was something to which he gave long and deliberate attention and that he delivered at least six times. His first delivery was for the Young Men's Association, in Centre Hall, Bloomington, Illinois, on April 6, 1858.[12] The local newspaper called Lincoln "an able and original thinker" who filled every seat in the hall at an early hour.[13] Lincoln spoke in Jacksonville, Illinois, on February 4, 1859, in Springfield, Illinois, on February 21, 1859, and in Decatur, Illinois, sometime in March that year.[14] His reappearance in Bloomington for an encore performance of his lecture on April 8, 1859, was so poorly attended that Lincoln did not speak, and the few attendees were refunded their admission fees.[15] The lone existing reminiscence of Lincoln's delivery in Pontiac, Illinois, on January 27, 1860, criticized his performance as disappointing and inferior, stating the talk itself was "on no particular subject and not well connected."[16] Lincoln's final performance of his lecture was on April 26, 1860, at Springfield, Illinois, before the Springfield Library Association in Cook's Hall.[17] His last delivery, similar to his first, was reported to have attracted a "large and intelligent audience" (probably due in part to his nationally acclaimed performance at Cooper Union in New York City only two months previously) and was praised as "of the most instructive and entertaining character."[18]

Despite the mixed reviews of his ability as lecturer, Lincoln continued to receive more invitations for talks, although he did not accept them all. He refused invitations to lecture in Galesburg and Rock Island, Illinois, in 1859, as well as in Philadelphia, Pennsylvania, in 1860, citing the pressure of legal business.[19] Lincoln certainly was pressured for time by 1860, having not only his legal career but also having gained national attention as a politician and possible presidential candidate. Lincoln never again expounded on the lecture circuit.

His interest in discoveries and inventions never abated, however, as shown in his great interest in new weapons and ordnance for the Union army during the war.[20] Even in a civilian capacity his interest continued. When Lincoln met Harvard professor Louis Agassiz in January 1865, he not only asked the scholar "how he studied—how he composed—how he delivered his lectures—how he found different tastes in his audiences, in different parts of the country, etc." but also talked about his lecture on discoveries and inventions, saying it was not quite perfected and that after his presidency he planned to work on it some more and perhaps have it published.[21]

Lincoln's continuous thoughts on his lecture, beginning with its inception in about 1849 and continuing into his presidency, shows that, to him, it was a serious and worthwhile endeavor and one that he wanted to finalize and share with the world in a published form. (This also was one of the main themes of his lecture—that the written word creates freedom and progress, and those words must be protected by patents, or copyrights.) As will be shown, not everyone agreed with Lincoln's own assessment of the lecture, however, including his son Robert and former secretary Nicolay.

The provenance of the actual physical documents on which Lincoln's lecture on discoveries and inventions was written has its own interesting history—a part of which has never before been realized or written. In Roy P. Basler's edition of Lincoln's collected works, the lecture is printed as two separate pieces: "First Lecture on Discoveries and Inventions," dated 1858, and "Second Lecture on Discoveries and Inventions," dated 1859. It was thought for decades that these were two separate lectures on the same topic, the first version being "completely rewritten" for its later delivery in 1859.[22] Lincoln scholar Wayne C. Temple, in his inimitable examination of the lecture, has shown that the two "versions" are actually the same speech, and the one Basler labels the "second" lecture most likely was the first part composed.[23]

Part of the confusion, according to Temple, comes from the misunderstanding by Dr. Samuel H. Melvin, a friend of Lincoln and resident of Springfield in 1861, who acquired the fragments from

Mary Lincoln's cousin Elizabeth Todd Grimsley (later also Brown).[24]
Melvin recounted his acquisition in a sworn affidavit.

> In the month of February, 1861, being at that time a resident
> of Springfield, Illinois, I called one evening at the residence
> of my friend, Dr. John Todd. The doctor was an uncle of Mrs.
> Abraham Lincoln. While there Mr. Lincoln came in, bring-
> ing with him a well-filled satchel, remarking as he set it down
> that it contained his literary bureau. Mr. Lincoln remained
> some fifteen or twenty minutes, conversing mainly about the
> details of his prospective trip to Washington the following
> week, and told us of the arrangements agreed upon for the
> family to follow him a few days later. When about to leave
> he handed the grip above referred to to Mrs. Grimsley, the
> only daughter of Dr. Todd, who was then a widow, but who
> subsequently became the wife of Rev. Dr. John H. Brown, a
> Presbyterian minister located in Springfield, remarking as he
> did so that he would leave the bureau in her charge; that if
> he ever returned to Springfield he would claim it, but if not
> she might make such disposition of its contents as she deemed
> proper. A tone of indescribable sadness was noted in the latter
> part of the sentence. Lincoln had shown me quite a number
> of letters a few days before, threatening his life, some predict-
> ing that he never would be inaugurated, and it was apparent
> to me that they were making an impression upon his mind,
> although he tried to laugh the matter off. About five years
> later the Nation was startled by the announcement of Lin-
> coln's assassination. The corporation of Springfield selected
> twelve of its citizens to proceed at once to Washington and
> accompany the remains of the dead President back to his old
> home. I was one of that number, and shall never forget the
> indescribable sadness manifested by millions of mourners along
> the route of travel of the funeral cortege as it wended its way
> westward over two thousand miles. A few evenings after his
> body was laid to rest, I again called upon my neighbors, the
> family of Dr. Todd. Scenes and incidents connected with the

assassination and funeral of the dead President were discussed, and the remark made by Lincoln on his last visit to the house was referred to as indicating a presentiment that he would not return alive. This recalled the fact of his having left his so-called literary bureau, and his injunction as to its disposition. Mrs. Grimsley brought the grip from the place where it had been stored, and opened it with a view to examining its contents. Among them was found this manuscript, and attached to it by means of a piece of red tape was another of like character. They proved to be manuscripts of two lectures which he had prepared and delivered within a year prior to his election to the presidency—one at Jacksonville, Illinois, and a few days later at Decatur, Illinois; the other a little later at Cook's Hall, Springfield, Illinois, at which I was present. Mrs. Grimsley told me to select from the contents of the bureau any one of the manuscripts it contained; and supposing at that time that the two manuscripts belonged to the same lecture, I selected them. On subsequent examination I discovered that while they both treated the same subject (Inventions and Discoveries) they were separate lectures. Twenty-five years later I disposed of one of the manuscripts to Mr. Gunther of Chicago. The other it is my hope and desire shall remain in possession of my family and its descendants.[25]

Despite the fact that Lincoln fastened the two fragments together with a piece of red tape, Melvin "jumped to a false assumption" that he had acquired two lectures, Temple asserts.[26]

As Melvin stated in his affidavit and Basler repeated in his editing of Lincoln's collected works, Melvin kept the "first" lecture but sold the "second" one to Charles Gunther, a Chicago collector, who sold it to prominent Lincoln collector Oliver R. Barrett.[27] "Thus, the error has been perpetuated, because no other scholar delved for any additional history of the manuscript," Temple concluded.[28] For decades, therefore, historians believed these two constituted all that existed of Lincoln's lecture. That they were not complete, but parts of the lecture, has been explained by scholars that Lincoln probably

We have all heard of Young America— He is the most current youth of the age— Some think him conceited, and arrogant; but has he not reason to entertain a rather extensive of mion of himself? Is he not the inventor and owner of the present, and sole hope of the future? Men, and things, everywhere are ministering unto him— Look at his apparel, and you shall see cotton fabrics from Manchester and Lowell; flax linen from Ireland; wool cloth for _____ silk from France; furs for the Arctic regions, with a buffalo robe for the Rocky Mountains, as a general outside At his table, besides plain bread and meat made at home, are sugar from Louisiana; coffee and fruits from the tropics; salt from Turk's Island; fish from New foundland; tea from China, and spices from the Indies— The whale of the Pacific furnishes his candle light; he has a diamond ring from Brazil, a gold watch from California, and a spanish cigar from Havana— He not only has a present supply of all these, and much more; but thousands of hands are engaged in producing fresh supplies, and other thousands, in bringing them to him— The iron horse is panting and impatient, to carry him everywhere, in no time; and the lightening stands ready harnessed to take and bring his tidings in a trifle less than no time He owns a large part of the world, by right of posses-

The beginning of what has been dubbed Abraham Lincoln's "Second Lecture on Discoveries and Inventions" is part of the copy that Dr. Samuel H. Melvin sold to Charles Gunther, who sold it to Lincoln collector Oliver R. Barrett. Alfred C. Berol donated it to Southern Illinois University in 1968. Photo courtesy Special Collections Research Center, Morris Library, Southern Illinois University Carbondale.

never finished the lecture but rather made these notes and extemporized parts of the speech as he spoke.[29] This argument is buttressed by statements made from numerous witnesses to Lincoln's delivery of his lecture who remarked on passages that are not written in either the "first" lecture or the "second."

Specifically, witnesses stated that Lincoln's lecture discussed the values of both laughter and music, with the former being the most frequently remembered. The *Bloomington* (Illinois) *Daily Pantagraph* reported that Lincoln's 1858 talk there "treated of and illustrated" laughter in his "own inimitable way" and that he also discussed music, which, "like flowers, was a gift of pure benevolence from our good Creator."[30] Nicolay remembered that the lecture he heard in Springfield in 1860 was "much longer" than the Gunther pages (the typically referenced version of the lecture before Basler's *Collected Works* was published in the early 1950s) and "contained several fine passages which made an impression on his memory; notably a reference to the importance and value of laughter, and a characterization of it as the 'joyous, universal, evergreen of life'"; Nicolay declared that because of their form and brevity, the Gunther pages are only a version of the original.[31] Herndon also recalled that when he heard the lecture, Lincoln "now and then . . . indulged in a humorous paragraph, and witticisms were freely sprinkled throughout."[32] Likewise, Ward Hill Lamon recalled that part of the lecture was "humorous," and "a very small part of it was actually witty."[33]

In light of this positive evidence for extra materials not in the lecture fragments and the lack of evidence concerning any other known copies of the lecture, the conclusion that Lincoln wrote only these notes and fragments and extemporized the rest differently at each appearance is logical, even inevitable. An examination of Lincoln's major speeches, however, (and the breadth, depth, and frequency of delivery of the lecture on discoveries and inventions allows it to be labeled a major effort) shows that he rarely, if ever, allowed himself impromptu remarks at such times; once he was nominated for president, his avoidance of ad-libbing was almost complete.[34] Is it possible, therefore, that Lincoln did write another version of the lecture, one that contained these references to laughter and music, one from which he either read as he lectured or composed later for his own posterity? And if so, what happened to that version? Previously neglected correspondence between Robert Lincoln and John Nicolay on this topic proves that indeed there was another version of this lecture, and, in fact, it was Abraham Lincoln's delivery copy. Even more interesting, Robert owned and subsequently lost the manuscript, and his attempts to find and reclaim it were unsuccessful.

After the murder of his father, Robert Lincoln became not only the owner but also the custodian of all his martyred father's papers. With the help of President Lincoln's secretaries Nicolay and Hay, Robert boxed all his father's political papers from the White House and sent them with Judge David Davis to be kept in Davis's safe in Bloomington, Illinois.[35] Robert also had personal family papers of his father in his own possession. In 1874, Robert entrusted his father's White House papers to Nicolay—then marshal of the U.S. Supreme Court—who had them stored in the United States Capitol. Nicolay and Hay organized and utilized these manuscripts in the composition of their great ten-volume biography of Abraham Lincoln and in their two-volume edition of Lincoln's collected works—both projects overseen and encouraged by Robert Lincoln.

Upon Nicolay's death in 1901, the Lincoln papers were transferred to the State Department under the supervision of Hay, who then was secretary of state. When Hay died in 1905, Robert again took the papers into his own possession and kept them with him at all times, bringing them, via special Pullman car (which, as president of the Pullman Car Company, Robert had at his disposal), between his different residences in Chicago, Georgetown, and Manchester, Vermont. In 1919, Robert had his papers stored in the Library of Congress for safekeeping—although he retained ownership and sole control over access—and eventually donated the papers in 1923 to the American people to be held in trust by the library.[36]

The history of the storage of the papers is important to know in order to understand the story of the lost version of Lincoln's lecture. In 1887, Nicolay and Hay were in the midst of composing their great Lincoln biography and already contemplating an edition of his collected works.[37] Nicolay was searching for Abraham Lincoln's lecture on discoveries and inventions to be included in both. Being unable to find it among the Lincoln papers under his care, Nicolay wrote to Robert Lincoln about it, but Robert was unsure of its location. "I do not remember having seen the manuscript for a long time and had a general idea you had it," Robert responded in October 1887.[38] After a thorough search of the papers in his home and law office, Robert could not find the manuscript anywhere. "I had no doubt it was in some box long closed up, but . . . it is nowhere to be found," he wrote Nicolay two months later. He remembered lending it to Isaac Arnold—a friend, colleague, and early biographer of Abraham Lincoln—to read but was sure it had been returned. "It was a mss book, thin, in black cover, evidently got for the purpose of copying the Lecture into it, as was done by my father in his own hand" and was "evidently the one used in delivery," Robert wrote.[39]

Robert Lincoln's reference to the missing lecture manuscript as a "book" handwritten by his father and used for delivery is an exciting revelation. No version of Lincoln's lecture transcribed in a bound book is known to exist, and no scholar has ever known what, if any, papers Lincoln actually read from during his "Discoveries and Inventions" speeches. It is known that the two fragments of the lecture, in loose pages, were given by Lincoln to Elizabeth Grimsley in 1861, which she then passed on to Samuel Melvin. That the manuscript was handwritten by Lincoln also is important in that for him to transcribe his lecture in a bound book certainly gives it an air of finality, or at least of serious consideration. Also, because this book was not left in Springfield with the other items in Elizabeth Grimsley's satchel, it is highly probable that it was taken by Lincoln to Washington—or created by him during his years as president. This likelihood adds a new layer to the history of Lincoln's lecture and of the degree to which he admired it and considered it a serious endeavor. It seemed to be his intention all along to seek its publication, as he had published his debates with Stephen Douglas, and so began this bound-book version sometime in 1860 to give it a more permanent composition. In 1865, he mentioned publication to Agassiz and said that he might try to publish it eventually after his presidency.

Another revelation in Robert's December 18, 1887 letter is that he never knew his father had given the loose pages to Lizzie Grimsley, or that, by 1887, Melvin owned them. "It is to me very odd that there should be another copy of it," Robert wrote. "My copy was evidently the one used in delivery and it is difficult to imagine why my father should have made another. It would be less strange if Melvin's mss was my missing book. There is no use in speculating when or how my copy left my possession for until now I did not for a moment think it had done so."[40] But the fragments owned by Melvin and, eventually, Charles Gunther, were different than the one Robert lost. As Robert wrote to Nicolay in December 1890, after having visited Gunther's shop and examined his copy of the lecture, "It consists of a few lines over thirteen pages of old-fashioned blue legal cap entirely autographic, but not signed or dated. . . . I may say here, that while it may be verbally the same as the one I lost, it is not the same paper, for mine was transcribed in a bound blank book, as perhaps you remember."[41]

Although Robert was certain that Isaac Arnold had returned the lecture book to him, he wrote to Arnold's daughter, Katherine, to ask her to search through her father's papers "in the mere chance, and to exhaust all means of discovery."[42] She searched, as she was asked, but could find no book of Lincoln's manuscript lecture.[43] "I cannot imagine what has become of the manuscript," Robert wrote to Nicolay in May 1889, while forwarding to him Katherine's letter.[44] Unfortunately for posterity and for Nicolay and Hay, Robert never found his lost book. Instead, he asked Charles Gunther to allow Nicolay and Hay to use his version in their biography and collected works of Lincoln. At first, Robert thought Gunther—whom he described as "an American collector of mummies, mss, pictures, hair, or anything"—to be a "good natured gentleman."[45] But once he met Gunther and told him of his interest in Nicolay and Hay's work, Robert found him to be not quite so amenable as he expected:

He spoke of the high price he paid for the manuscript (I may say to you confidentially, because he told it to me so, that he paid $250 for it,) and he evidently had in mind some idea of making money out of it. He spoke of his intention of having it printed in pamphlet form and copyrighted, the copies to be sold at the Libby Prison Museum here [in Chicago], in which he is interested. It was very difficult to keep him down to the business at hand, because one large floor of his business place is entirely filled with what he calls historical curiosities, some of them really interesting, many of them very trashy, and if you will not quote me, I will express my opinion, that he sees no great difference and interest between a worn out royal tooth brush and an original copy of the Magna Carta, if he had it. All such things are on a common plane to him and he was constantly interrupting my talk to show me and expatiate on some piece of nonsense in his collection which would occur to him. I tried in vain, to get him to do more than say he would think the matter over and would write you, if you would write to him, so I suppose there is nothing else but for you to do this.[46]

Nicolay eventually secured Gunther's permission to use his copy of the lecture and used it both in an 1894 *Century Magazine* article about Lincoln's writing and in his and Hay's collected works of Abraham Lincoln.[47]

Yet, despite this three-year search for the lecture by Robert and Nicolay in order to include it in Lincoln's collected works, neither man thought very highly of the speech itself. Robert Lincoln thought the lecture to seem "out of place" among his father's writings of the late 1850s and called it, "in a sense, the solemn recording of a piece of play, the only visible break in a long current of serious work upon the one subject that really engaged his attention in that period." Believing that even his father did not regard the lecture very seriously, he wondered to Nicolay in December 1890, if including it in the collected works would "excite an utterly undeserved attention and criticism, and indeed as nearly everything else you can have has already been long known, it may excite undivided attention, and the carelessly unjust criticism of the newspapers of the day, paying no attention to the circumstances of the case." Here we see the rearing of Robert Lincoln's famous aversion to publicity and zealous protection of his father's legacy, a trait that showed itself in previous years and would continue to do so until his death in 1926. But in the end, Robert told Nicolay that those were "simply my notions, not intended to over-ride any matured ideas on the subject you and Hay may have."[48]

Always deferential to Robert in matters regarding his father, Nicolay responded, "Your estimate of [the lecture] is entirely just and we had no idea of parading it as a serious piece of literary work, but to class it among a few miscellanea and thus, since it must invariably become public, to ourselves put its proper and subordinate stamp upon it."[49] He and Hay did include it in their collected works, but merely as a transcript of the Gunther copy and a note as to two dates of its delivery. Nicolay also mentioned it and transcribed it in his 1894 article but declared it to be "unjust to devote any serious criticism" to it since it "must be regarded in the light of mere recreation to satisfy the craving for a change from the monotony of law and politics"—a sentiment decidedly similar to Robert's opinion in his previous letter to Nicolay.[50]

Over the years, Lincoln's lecture on discoveries and inventions has been typically overlooked when placed within the catalog of Lincoln's great writings and speeches, for being, what one scholar dubbed, "anomalous."[51] Herndon called it "commonplace" and said it "met with the disapproval of his friends, and he himself was filled with disgust."[52] Basler called the lecture "a somewhat colorless disquisition" that Lincoln "never thought much of it, and in truth it did not measure up to his other nonpolitical address delivered before the Wisconsin State Agricultural Fair on September 30, 1859."[53] Pulitzer Prize–winning author Garry Wills, on the other hand, in his incomparable study of Lincoln's Gettysburg Address, called the lecture on discoveries and inventions a "mature speech . . . reworked and seriously considered at the peak of his political life."[54]

Since the turn of the twenty-first century, at least two scholars have undertaken thorough critical examinations of Lincoln's lecture and determined it to have a much more trenchant and immediate value than previously considered. In 2001, scholar Eugene F. Miller, professor of political science at the University of Georgia, examined Lincoln's lecture for the political principles it espoused, namely, its promotion of technological advance to further democratic values. "His interest in discoveries and inventions fits well with his long-standing efforts to foster economic development," Miller asserted. "Moreover, the lecture speaks to a question that is vital to the debate about slavery, that is, whether technological advance tends in the long run to strengthen slavery or to defeat it. Lincoln's reflections on discoveries and inventions, far from being of peripheral interest, serve to draw together two of his longstanding concerns: issues of economics and issues of slavery."[55] Miller's exegesis is an impressive and valuable political critique of a lecture long thought dissociated from Lincoln's political ideology.

In 2005, John Channing Briggs, a professor of English at the University of California, Riverside, undertook a critical literary analysis of Lincoln's lecture and showed, among other things, how its correlation to Lincoln's speech at the 1859 Wisconsin State Agricultural Fair, negates the notion that the discoveries lecture was "merely a passing whimsy." Briggs also points out—serving as a concomitant point to Miller's thesis—that the multiple deliveries of Lincoln's discoveries lectures from 1858 to 1860 came in a period of political activity that was "especially intense," and his language in both that speech and the one to the Wisconsin State Agricultural Fair was "dense with political meanings." Yet, Briggs can't help but ask, "What was it about Lincoln's humble attempt at lecturing on discoveries and inventions that kept him thinking about elaborating what he had said?" Briggs concludes, "The discoveries lecture seems to have supplied a balancing countermovement during a period of personal defeat and triumph—an opportunity to delve into philosophical issues not bound by immediate political imperatives, yet containing deep political ramifications in a time of crisis."[56] Briggs's insightful examination, like Miller's, illuminates and elucidates Lincoln's lecture to a degree not previously accomplished and shows that it neither was a wasted intellectual effort by Lincoln nor is it a wasted historical effort by contemporary scholars to pay it more attention.

Indeed, as generations, technologies, and general perspectives change—as well as with the renaissance of Lincoln studies with the bicentennial on February 12, 2009, of his birth—Lincoln's lecture on discoveries and inventions continues to take on new meanings and new importance. Historians have revealed how Lincoln conceived of the lecture, how he wrote it, where he delivered it, what he considered its value, and what he planned to do with it after his presidency. The lecture has been analyzed for its literary, oratorical, political, and social insights and values. The one question that has always remained is why only pieces of it were left, despite Lincoln's having delivered it six times. As the correspondence between Robert Lincoln and John Nicolay shows, there was at least one more version of this lecture, bound in a book, that has been lost to history. Whether this was a more finalized version of the lecture is unclear, but this new knowledge adds another piece to the puzzle of the seemingly unfinished lecture and creates another insight—however small—into one more piece of Lincoln's life. It also proves that despite wonders and worries about whether the Lincoln theme has been exhausted, unknown facts about the life and work of Abraham Lincoln continue to be uncovered.

ACKNOWLEDGMENTS

APPENDIXES

NOTES

BIBLIOGRAPHY

INDEX

ACKNOWLEDGMENTS

Special thanks to Wayne C. Temple, the first Lincoln scholar to truly plumb the depths of this topic, for sharing his knowledge of the subject with me; to Harry R. Rubenstein, chair, Division of Politics and Reform, Smithsonian Institution, for allowing me the amazing experience of seeing Lincoln's original patent model and discussing with me his knowledge of it; to Daniel W. Stowell, director and editor of the Papers of Abraham Lincoln, for his aid with identifying a patent case; to Phil Wagner, publisher, for allowing me to use the original artwork of the late Lloyd Ostendorf; to my friend Tom Byrnes for designing a great cover; and to my editor, Sylvia Frank Rodrigue, for believing in the possibility of this book.

UNITED STATES PATENT OFFICE

ABRAHAM LINCOLN, OF SPRINGFIELD, ILLINOIS.

BUOYING VESSELS OVER SHOALS.

Specification forming part of Letters Patent No. 6,469, dated May 22, 1849; application filed March 10, 1849.

To all whom it may concern:

Be it known that I, Abraham Lincoln, of Springfield, in the County of Sangamon, in the State of Illinois, have invented a new and improved manner of combining adjustable buoyant air chambers with a steamboat or other vessel for the purpose of enabling their draught of water to be readily lessened to enable them to pass over bars, or through shallow water, without discharging their cargoes; and I do hereby declare the following to be a full, clear, and exact description thereof, reference being had to the accompanying drawings making a part of this specification. Similar letters indicate like parts in all the figures.

The buoyant chambers A, A, which I employ, are constructed in such a manner that they can be expanded so as to hold a large volume of air when required for use, and can be contracted, into a very small space and safely secured as soon as their services can be dispensed with.

Fig. 1, is a side elevation of a vessel with the buoyant chambers combined therewith, expanded;

Fig. 2, is a transverse section of the same with the buoyant chambers contracted.

Fig. 3, is a longitudinal vertical section through the centre of one of the buoyant chambers, and the box B, for receiving it when contracted, which is secured to the lower guard of the vessel.

The top g, and bottom h, of each buoyant chamber, is composed of plank or metal, of suitable strength and stiffness, and the flexible sides and ends of the chambers, are composed of india-rubber cloth, or other suitable water-proof fabric, securely united to the edges and ends of the top and bottom of the chambers.

The sides of the chambers may be stayed and supported centrally by a frame k, as shown in Fig. 3, or as many stays may be combined with them as may be necessary to give them the requisite fullness and strength when expanded.

The buoyant chambers are suspended and operated as follows: A suitable number of vertical shafts or spars D, D, are combined with each of the chambers, as represented in Figs. 2 and 3, to wit: The shafts work freely in apertures formed in the upper sides of the chambers, and their lower ends are permanently secured to the under sides of the chambers: The vertical shafts or spars (D,D,) pass up through the top of the boxes B, B, on the lower guards of the vessel, and then through its upper guards, or some other suitable support, to keep them in a vertical position.

The vertical shafts (D, D,) are connected to the main shaft C, which passes longitudinally through the centre of the vessel—just below its upper deck—by endless ropes $f, f,$ as represented in Fig. 2: The said ropes, $f, f,$ being wound several times around the main shaft C, then passing outwards over sheaves or rollers attached to the upper deck or guards of the vessel, from which they descend along the inner sides of the vertical shafts or spars D, D, to sheaves or rollers connected to the boxes B, B, and thence rise to the main shaft (C,) again.

The ropes $f, f,$ are connected to the vertical shafts at $i, i,$ as shown in Figs. 1 and 2. It will therefore be perceived, that by turning the main shaft C, in one direction, the buoyant chambers will be expanded into the position shown in Fig. 1; and by turning the shaft in an opposite direction, the chambers will be contracted into the position shown in Fig. 2.

In Fig. 3, $e, e,$ are check ropes, made fast to the tops of the boxes B, B, and to the upper sides of the buoyant chambers; which ropes catch and retain the upper sides of the chambers when their lower sides are forced down, and cause the chambers to be expanded to their full capacity. By varying the length of the check ropes, the depth of immersion of the buoyant chambers can be governed. A suitable number of openings $m, m,$ are formed in the upper sides of the buoyant chambers, for the admission and emission of air when the chambers are expanded and contracted.

The ropes $f, f,$ that connect the main shaft C, with the shafts or spars D, D, (rising from the buoyant chambers,) may be passed from one to the other in any direction that may be deemed best, and that will least incommode the deck of the vessel; or other mechanical means may be employed as the medium of communication between the main shaft and the buoyant chambers, if it should be found expedient.

I shall generally make the main shaft C, in as many parts as there are corresponding pairs of buoyant chambers, so that by coupling the sections of the shaft together, the whole of the chambers can be expanded at the same time, and by disconnecting them, either pair of chambers can be expanded, separately from the others as circumstances may require.

The buoyant chambers may be operated by the power of the steam engine applied to the main shaft C. in any convenient manner, or by man power.

Where the guards of a vessel are very high above the water, the boxes B, B, for the reception of the buoyant chambers when contracted, may be dispensed with, and the chambers be contracted by drawing them against the under side of the guards. Or, protecting cases may be secured to the under sides of the guards for the reception of the buoyant chambers when contracted.

When it is desired to combine my expansible buoyant chambers with vessels which have no projecting guards; shelves or cases must be strongly secured to their sides for the reception of the buoyant chambers.

I wish it to be distinctly understood, that I do not intend to limit myself to any particular mechanical arrangement, in combining expansible buoyant chambers with a vessel, but shall vary the same as I may deem expedient, whilst I attain the same end by substantially the same means.

What I claim as my invention and desire to secure by letters patent, is the combination of expansible buoyant chambers placed at the sides of a vessel, with the main shaft or shafts C, by means of the sliding spars or shafts D, which pass down through the buoyant chambers and are made fast to their bottoms, and the series of ropes and pullies, or their equivalents, in such a manner that by turning the main shaft or shafts in one direction, the buoyant chambers will be forced downwards into the water and at the same time expanded and filled with air for buoying up the vessel by the displacement of water; and by turning the shaft in an opposite direction, the buoyant chambers will be contracted into a small space and secured against injury.

A. LINCOLN.

Witness:
  Z. C. ROBBINS,
  H. H. SYLVESTER.

ABRAHAM LINCOLN

MANNER OF BOUYING VESSELS

No. 6,469

Patented May 22, 1849

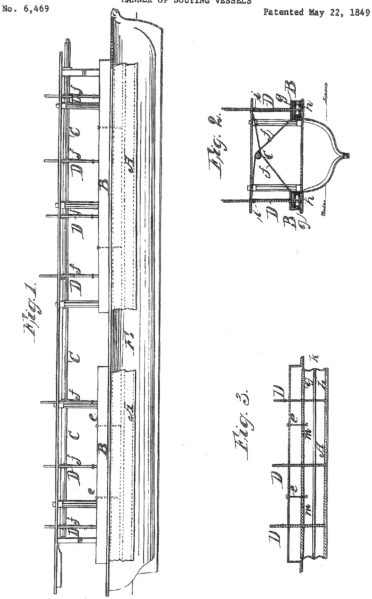

APPENDIX 2: LINCOLN'S FIRST AND SECOND LECTURES ON DISCOVERIES AND INVENTIONS

The text and endnotes of Lincoln's lecture on discoveries and inventions are reprinted from *The Collected Works of Abraham Lincoln*, edited by Roy P. Basler with the assistance of Marion Dolores Pratt and Lloyd A. Dunlap, 9 vols. (New Brunswick, NJ: Rutgers University Press, 1953–55); the first lecture is from 2:437–42 and the second from 3:356–63. The second lecture, an autograph, was in the Oliver R. Barrett Collection, which in 1952 was sold and dispersed among several collections (Basler, *Collected Works*, viii). Misspellings, misuses of grammar, and some punctuation—due mostly to their nineteenth-century origins—have been changed without the use of *sic*, which the current author finds annoying and interruptive to the narrative flow. No other editing has been undertaken. In the second lecture, the uses of square brackets are the editorial insertions of Basler.

First Lecture on Discoveries and Inventions
April 6, 1858

All creation is a mine, and every man, a miner.[1]

The whole earth, and all *within* it, *upon* it, and *round about* it, including *himself*, in his physical, moral, and intellectual nature, and his susceptibilities, are the infinitely various "leads" from which, man, from the first, was to dig out his destiny.

In the beginning, the mine was unopened, and the miner stood *naked*, and *knowledgeless*, upon it.

Fishes, birds, beasts, and creeping things, are not miners, but *feeders* and *lodgers*, merely. Beavers build houses; but they build them in no wise differently, or better now, than they did, five thousand years ago. Ants, and honey-bees, provide food for winter; but just in the *same way* they did, when Solomon referred the sluggard to them as patterns of prudence.[2]

Man is not the only animal who labors; but he is the only one who *improves* his workmanship. This improvement, he effects by *Discoveries* and *Inventions*. His first important discovery was the fact that he was naked; and his first invention was the fig-leaf-apron. This simple article—the apron—made of leaves, seems to have been the origin of *clothing*—the one thing for which nearly half of the toil and care of the human race has ever since been expended. The most important improvement ever made in connection with clothing, was the invention of *spinning* and *weaving*. The spinning jenny, and power-loom, invented in modern times, though great *improvements*, do not, as *inventions*, rank with the ancient arts of spinning and weaving. Spinning and weaving brought into the department of clothing such abundance and variety of material. Wool, the hair of several species of animals, hemp, flax, cotton, silk, and perhaps other articles, were all suited to it, affording garments not only adapted to wet and dry, heat and cold, but also susceptible of high degrees of ornamental finish. Exactly *when*, or *where*, spinning and weaving originated is not known. At the first interview of the Almighty with Adam and Eve, after the fall, He made "coats of skins, and clothed them" Gen: 3:21.

The Bible makes no other allusion to clothing, *before* the flood. Soon *after* the deluge Noah's two sons covered him with a *garment*; but of what *material* the garment was made is not mentioned. Gen. 9:23.

Abraham mentions "*thread*" in such connection as to indicate that spinning and weaving were in use in his day—Gen. 14:23—and soon after, reference to the art is frequently made. "*Linen breeches,*["] are mentioned,—Exod. 28:42—and it is said "all the women that were wise hearted, did *spin* with their hands" (35:25) and, "all the women whose hearts stirred them up in wisdom, *spun* goat's hair" (35:26). The work of the "*weaver*" is mentioned—(35:35). In the book of Job, a very old book, date not exactly known, the "*weavers shuttle*" is mentioned.

The above mention of "*thread*" by Abraham is the oldest recorded allusion to spinning and weaving; and *it* was made about two thousand years after the creation of man, and now, near four thousand years ago. Profane authors think these arts originated in Egypt; and this is not contradicted, or made improbable, by any thing in the Bible; for the allusion of Abraham, mentioned, was not made until after he had sojourned in Egypt.

The discovery of the properties of *iron*, and the making of *iron tools*, must have been among the earliest of important discoveries and inventions. We can scarcely conceive the possibility of making much of anything else, without the use of iron tools. Indeed, an *iron hammer* must have been very much needed to make the *first* iron hammer with. A *stone* probably served as a substitute. How could the "*gopher wood*" for the Ark, have been gotten out without an axe? It seems to me an axe, or a miracle, was indispensable. Corresponding with the prime necessity for iron, we find at least one very early notice of it. Tubal-cain was "an instructer of every artificer in *brass* and *iron*["]—Gen. 4:22. Tubal-cain was the seventh in descent from Adam; and his birth was about one thousand years before the flood. *After* the flood, frequent mention is made of *iron*, and *instruments* made of iron. Thus "instrument of iron" at Num: 35:16; "bed-stead of iron" at Deut. 3:11—"the iron furnace ["] at 4:20—and "iron tool" at 27:5. At 19:5—very distinct mention of "the ax to cut down the tree" is made; and also at 8:9, the promised land is described as "a land whose stones are iron, and out of whose hills thou mayest dig brass." From the somewhat frequent mention of brass in connection with iron, it is not improbable that brass—perhaps what we now call copper—was used by the ancients for some of the same purposes as iron.

Transportation—the removal of person, and goods—from place to place—would be an early *object*, if not a *necessity*, with man. By his natural powers of locomotion, and without much assistance from Discovery and invention, he could move himself about with considerable facility; and even, could carry small burthens with him. But very soon he would wish to lessen the labor, while he might, at the same time, extend, and expedite the business. For this object, wheel-carriages, and water-crafts—wagons and boats—are the most important inventions. The use of the wheel & axle, has been so long known, that it is difficult, without reflection, to estimate it at its true value.[3]

The oldest recorded allusion to the wheel and axle is the mention of a "chariot" Gen. 41:43. This was in Egypt, upon the occasion of Joseph being made Governor by Pharaoh. It was about twenty-five hundred years after the creation of Adam. That the chariot then mentioned was a wheel-carriage drawn by animals, is sufficiently evidenced by the mention of chariot-*wheels*, at Exod. 14:25, and the mention of chariots in connection with *horses*, in the same chapter, verses 9 & 23. So much, at present, for land-transportation.

Now, as to transportation by *water*, I have concluded, without sufficient authority perhaps, to use the term "boat" as a general name for all watercraft. The boat is indispensable to navigation. It is not probable that the philosophical principle upon which the use of the boat primarily depends—to wit, the *principle*, that any thing will float, which can not sink without displacing more than its own *weight* of water—was known, or even thought of, before the first boats were made. The sight of a crow standing on a piece of drift-wood floating down the swollen current of a creek or river, might well enough suggest the specific idea to a savage, that he could himself get upon a log, or on two logs tied together, and somehow work his way to the opposite shore of the same stream. Such a suggestion, so taken, would be the birth of navigation; and such, not improbably, it really was. The leading idea was thus caught; and whatever came afterwards, were but improvements upon, and auxiliaries to, it.

As man is a land animal, it might be expected he would learn to travel by land somewhat earlier than he would by water. Still the crossing of streams, somewhat too deep for wading, would be an early necessity with him. If we pass by the Ark, which may be regarded as belonging rather to the *miraculous*, than to *human* invention the first notice we have of watercraft, is the mention of "ships" by Jacob— Gen. 49:13. It is not till we reach the book of Isaiah that we meet with the mention of "oars" and "sails."

As man's *food*—his first necessity—was to be derived from the vegetation of the earth, it was natural that his first care should be directed to the assistance of that vegetation. And accordingly we find that, even before the fall, the man was put into the garden of Eden "to dress it, and to keep it." And when afterwards, in consequence of the first transgression, *labor* was imposed on the race, as a *penalty*—a *curse*—we find the first-born man—the first heir of the curse—was "a tiller of the ground." This was the beginning of agriculture; and although, both in point of time, and of importance, it stands at the head of all branches of human industry, it has derived less direct advantage from Discovery and Invention, than almost any other. The plow, of very early origin; and reaping, and threshing, machines, of modern invention are, at this day, the principle improvements in agriculture. And even the oldest of these, the plow, could not have been conceived of, until a precedent conception had been caught, and put into practice—I mean the conception, or idea, of substituting other forces in nature, for man's own muscular power. These other forces, as now used, are principally, the *strength* of animals, and the *power* of the wind, of running streams, and of steam.

Climbing upon the back of an animal, and making it carry us, might not, occur very readily. I think the back of the camel would never have suggested it. It was, however, a matter of vast importance.

The earliest instance of it mentioned, is when "Abraham rose up early in the morning, and saddled his ass,["] Gen. 22:3 preparatory to sacrificing Isaac as a burnt-offering; but the allusion to the *saddle* indicates that riding had been in use some time; for it is quite probable they rode bare-backed awhile, at least, before they invented saddles.

The *idea*, being once conceived, of riding one species of animals, would soon be extended to others. Accordingly we find that when the servant of Abraham went in search of a wife for Isaac, he took ten *camels* with him; and, on his return trip, "Rebekah arose, and her damsels, and they rode upon the camels, and followed the man" Gen. 24:61[.]

The *horse*, too, as a riding animal, is mentioned early. The Red sea being safely passed, Moses and the children of Israel sang to the Lord "the *horse*, and his *rider* hath he thrown into the sea." Exo. 15:1.

Seeing that animals could bear *man* upon their backs, it would soon occur that they could also bear other burthens. Accordingly we find that Joseph's bretheren, on their first visit to Egypt, "laded their asses with the corn, and departed thence" Gen. 42:26.

Also it would occur that animals could be made to *draw* burthens *after* them, as well as to bear them upon their backs; and hence plows and chariots came into use early enough to be often mentioned in the books of Moses—Deut. 22:10. Gen. 41:43. Gen. 46:29. Exo. 14:25[.]

Of all the forces of nature, I should think the *wind* contains the largest amount of *motive power*—that is, power to move things. Take any given space of the earth's surface—for instance, Illinois—and all the power exerted by all the men, and beasts, and running-water, and steam, over and upon it, shall not equal the one hundredth part of what is exerted by the blowing of the wind over and upon the same space. And yet it has not, so far in the world's history, become proportionably *valuable* as a motive power. It is applied extensively, and advantageously, to sail-vessels in navigation. Add to this a few windmills, and pumps, and you have about all. That, as yet, no very successful mode of *controlling*, and *directing* the wind, has been discovered; and that, naturally, it moves by fits and starts—now so gently as to scarcely stir a leaf, and now so roughly as to level a forest—doubtless have been the insurmountable difficulties. As yet, the wind is an *untamed*, and *unharnessed* force; and quite possibly one of the greatest discoveries hereafter to be made, will be the taming, and harnessing of the wind. That the difficulties of controlling this power are very great is quite evident by the fact th at they have already been perceived, and struggled with more than three thousand years; for that power was applied to sail-vessels, at least as early as the time of the prophet Isaiah.

In speaking of *running streams*, as a motive power, I mean its application to mills and other machinery by means of the "*water wheel*"— a thing now well known, and extensively used; but, of which, no mention is made in the bible, though it is thought to have been in use among the Romans—(Am. Ency. tit—Mill)[.] The language of the Savior "Two women shall be grinding at the mill &c" indicates that, even in the populous city of Jerusalem, at that day, mills were operated by hand—having, as yet had no other than human power applied to them.

The advantageous use of *Steam-power* is, unquestionably, a modern discovery.

And yet, as much as two thousand years ago the power of steam was not only observed, but an ingenious toy was actually made and put in motion by it, at Alexandria in Egypt.

What appears strange is, that neither the inventor of the toy, nor any one else, for so long a time afterwards, should perceive that steam would move *useful* machinery as well as a toy.[4]

Second Lecture on Discoveries and Inventions
February 11, 1859

We have all heard of Young America.[5] He is the most *current* youth of the age. Some think him conceited, and arrogant; but has he not reason to entertain a rather extensive opinion of himself? Is he not the inventor and owner of the *present*, and sole hope of the *future*? Men, and things, everywhere, are ministering unto him. Look at his apparel, and you shall see cotton fabrics from Manchester and Lowell; flax-linen from Ireland; wool-cloth from [Spain;][6] silk from France; furs from the Arctic regions, with a buffalo robe from the Rocky Mountains, as a general out-sider. At his table, besides plain bread and meat made at home, are sugar from Louisiana; coffee and fruits from the tropics; salt from Turk's Island; fish from Newfoundland; tea from China, and spices from the Indies. The whale of the Pacific furnishes his candlelight; he has a diamond-ring from Brazil; a gold-watch from California, and a Spanish cigar from Havana. He not only has a present supply of all these, and much more; but thousands of hands are engaged in producing fresh supplies, and other thousands, in bringing them to him. The iron horse is panting, and impatient, to carry him everywhere, in no time; and the lightning stands ready harnessed to take and bring his tidings in a trifle less than no time. He owns a large part of the world, by right of possessing it; and all the rest by right of *wanting* it, and *intending* to have it. As Plato had for the immortality of the soul, so Young America has "a pleasing hope—a fond desire—a longing after" territory. He has a great passion—a perfect rage—for the "*new*"; particularly new men for office, and the new earth mentioned in the revelations, in which, being no more sea, there must be about three times as much land as in the present. He is a great friend of humanity; and his desire for land is not selfish, but merely an impulse to extend the area of freedom. He is very anxious to fight for the liberation of enslaved nations and colonies, provided, always, they *have* land, and have *not* any liking for his interference. As to those who have no land, and would be glad of help from any quarter, he considers *they* can afford to wait a few hundred years longer. In knowledge he is particularly rich. He knows all that can possibly be known, inclines to believe in spiritual rappings, and is the unquestioned inventor of *"Manifest Destiny."* His horror is for all that is old, particularly "Old Fogy"; and if there be any thing old which he can endure, it is only old whiskey and old tobacco.

If the said Young America really is, as he claims to be, the owner of all present, it must be admitted that he has considerable advantage of Old Fogy. Take, for instance, the first of all fogies, father Adam. There he stood, a very perfect physical man, as poets and painters inform us; but he must have been very ignorant, and simple in his habits. He had had no sufficient time to learn much by observation; and he had no near neighbors to teach him anything. No part of his breakfast had been brought from the other side of the world; and it is quite probable, he had no conception of the world having any other side. In all of these things, it is very plain, he was no equal of Young America; the most that can be said is, that *according to his chance* he may have been quite as much of a man as his very self-complaisant descendant. Little as was what he knew, let the Youngster discard all he has learned from others, and then show, if he can, any advantage on his side. In the way of *land*, and *livestock*, Adam was quite in the ascendant. He had dominion over all the earth, and all the living things upon, and round about it. The land has been sadly divided out since; but never fret, Young America will *re-annex* it.

The great difference between Young America and Old Fogy, is the result of *Discoveries, Inventions,* and *Improvements.* These, in turn, are the result of *observation, reflection,* and *experiment.* For instance, it is quite certain that ever since water has been boiled in covered vessels, men have seen the lids of the vessels rise and fall a little, with a sort of fluttering motion, by force of the steam; but so long as this was not specially observed, and reflected and experimented upon, it came to nothing. At length however, after many thousand years, some man observes this long-known effect of hot water lifting a pot-lid, and begins a train of reflection upon it. He says, "Why, to be sure, the force that lifts the pot-lid, will lift any thing else, which is no heavier than the pot-lid. And, as man has much hard lifting to do, can not this hot-water power be made to help him?" He has become a little excited on the subject, and he fancies he hears a voice answering, "Try me." He does try it; and the *observation*, *reflection*, and *trial* give to the world the control of that tremendous, and now well-known agent, called steam-power. This is not the actual history in detail, but the general principle.

But was this first inventor of the application of steam, wiser or more ingenious than those who had gone before him? Not at all. Had he not learned much of them, he never would have succeeded— probably, never would have thought of making the attempt. To be fruitful in invention, it is indispensable to have a *habit* of observation and reflection; and this *habit*, our steam friend acquired, no doubt, from those who, to him, were old fogies. But for the difference in *habit* of observation, why did yankees, almost instantly, discover gold in California, which had been trodden upon, and over-looked by Indians and Mexican greasers, for centuries? Gold mines are not the only mines overlooked in the same way. There are more mines above the Earth's surface than below it. All nature—the whole world, material, moral, and intellectual,—is a mine; and, in Adam's day, it was a wholly unexplored mine. Now, it was the destined work of Adam's race to develop, by discoveries, inventions, and improvements, the hidden treasures of this mine. But Adam had nothing to turn his attention to the work. If he should do anything in the way of invention, he had first to invent the art of invention—the *instance* at least, if not the *habit* of observation and reflection. As might be expected he seems not to have been a very observing man at first; for it appears he went about naked a considerable length of time, before he even noticed that obvious fact. But when he did observe it, the observation was not lost upon him; for it immediately led to the first of all inventions, of which we have any direct account—*the fig-leaf apron.*

The inclination to exchange thoughts with one another is probably an original impulse of our nature. If I be in pain I wish to let you know it, and to ask your sympathy and assistance; and my pleasurable emotions also, I wish to communicate to, and share with you. But to carry on such communication, some *instrumentality* is indispensable. Accordingly speech—articulate sounds rattled off from the tongue— was used by our first parents, and even by Adam, before the creation of Eve. He gave names to the animals while she was still a bone in his side; and he broke out quite volubly when she first stood before him, the best present of his maker. From this it would appear that speech was not an invention of man, but rather the direct gift of his Creator. But whether Divine gift, or invention, it is still plain that if a mode of communication had been left to invention, *speech* must have been the first, from the superior adaptation to the end, of the organs of speech, over every other means within the whole range of nature. Of the organs of speech the tongue is the principal; and if we shall test it, we shall find the capacities of the tongue, in the utterance of articulate sounds, absolutely wonderful. You can count from one to one hundred, quite distinctly in about forty seconds. In doing this, two hundred and eighty three distinct sounds or syllables are uttered, being seven to each second; and yet there shall be enough difference between every two, to be easily recognized by the ear of the hearer. What other *signs* to represent *things* could possibly be produced so rapidly? or, even, if ready made, could be *arranged* so rapidly to express the sense? *Motions* with the hands, are no adequate substitute. *Marks* for the recognition of the eye—*writing*—although a wonderful auxiliary for speech, are no worthy substitute for it. In addition to the more slow and laborious process of getting up a communication in writing, the materials—pen, ink, and paper—are not always at hand. But one always has his tongue with him, and the breath of his life is the ever-ready material with which it works. Speech, then, by enabling different individuals to interchange thoughts, and thereby to combine their powers of observation and reflection, greatly facilitates useful discoveries and inventions. What one observes, and would himself infer nothing from, he tells to another, and that other at once sees a valuable hint in it. A result is thus reached which neither *alone* would have arrived at.

And this reminds me of what I passed unnoticed before, that the very first invention was a joint operation, Eve having shared with Adam in the getting up of the apron. And, indeed, judging from the fact that sewing has come down to our times as "woman's work," it is very probable she took the leading part; he, perhaps, doing no more than to stand by and thread the needle. That proceeding may be reckoned as the mother of all "sewing societies"; and the first and most perfect "world's fair" all inventions and all inventors then in the world, being on the spot.

But speech alone, valuable as it ever has been, and is, has not advanced the condition of the world much. This is abundantly evident when we look at the degraded condition of all those tribes of human creatures who have no considerable additional means of communicating thoughts. *Writing*—the art of communicating thoughts to the mind, through the eye—is the great invention of the world. Great in the astonishing range of analysis and combination which necessarily underlies the most crude and general conception of it—great, very great in enabling us to converse with the dead, the absent, and the unborn, at all distances of time and of space; and great, not only in its direct benefits, but greatest help, to all other inventions. Suppose the art, with all conception of it, were this day lost to the world, how long, think you, would it be, before even Young America could get up the letter *A* with any adequate notion of using it to advantage? The precise period at which writing was invented, is not known; but it certainly was as early as the time of Moses; from which we may safely infer that its inventors were very old fogies.

Webster, at the time of writing his dictionary, speaks of the English Language as then consisting of seventy or eighty thousand words. If so, the language in which the five books of Moses were written must, at that time, now thirty-three or four hundred years ago, have consisted of at least one quarter as many, or, twenty thousand. When we remember that words are *sounds* merely, we shall conclude that the idea of representing those sounds by *marks*, so that whoever should at any time after see the marks, would understand what sounds they meant, was a bold and ingenious conception, not likely to occur to one man of a million, in the run of a thousand years. And, when it did occur, a distinct mark for each word, giving twenty thousand different marks first to be learned, and afterwards remembered, would follow as the second thought, and would present such a difficulty as would lead to the conclusion that the whole thing was impracticable. But the *necessity* still would exist; and we may readily suppose that the idea was conceived, and lost, and reproduced, and dropped, and taken up again and again, until at last, the thought of dividing sounds into parts, and making a mark, not to represent a whole sound, but only a part of one, and then of combining these marks, not very many in number, upon the principles of permutation, so as to represent any and all of the whole twenty thousand words, and even any additional number was somehow conceived and pushed into practice. This was the invention of *phonetic* writing, as distinguished from the clumsy picture writing of some of the nations. That it was difficult of conception and execution, is apparent, as well by the foregoing reflections, as by the fact that so many tribes of men have come down from Adam's time to ours without ever having possessed it. Its utility may be conceived, by the reflection that, to *it* we owe everything which distinguishes us from savages. Take it from us, and the Bible, all history, all science, all government, all commerce, and nearly all social intercourse go with it.

The great activity of the tongue, in articulating sounds, has already been mentioned; and it may be of some passing interest to notice the wonderful powers of the *eye*, in conveying ideas to the mind from writing. Take the same example of the numbers from *one* to *one hundred*, written down, and you can run your eye over the list, and be assured that every number is in it, in about one half the time it would require to pronounce the words with the voice; and not only so, but you can, in the same short time, determine whether every word is spelled correctly, by which it is evident that every separate letter, amounting to eight hundred and sixty-four, has been recognized, and reported to the mind, within the incredibly short space of twenty seconds, or one third of a minute.

I have already intimated my opinion that in the world's history, certain inventions and discoveries occurred, of peculiar value, on account of their great efficiency in facilitating all other inventions and discoveries. Of these were the arts of writing and of printing—the discovery of America, and the introduction of Patent-laws. The date of the first, as already stated, is unknown; but it certainly was as much as fifteen hundred years before the Christian era; the second—printing—came in 1436, or nearly three thousand years after the first. The others followed more rapidly—the discovery of America in 1492, and the first patent laws in 1624. Though not apposite to my present purpose, it is but justice to the fruitfulness of that period, to mention two other important events—the Lutheran Reformation in 1517, and, still earlier, the invention of negroes, or, of the present mode of using them, in 1434. But, to return to the consideration of printing, it is plain that it is but the *other* half—and in real utility, the *better* half—of writing; and that both together are but the assistants of speech in the communication of thoughts between man and man. When man was possessed of speech alone, the chances of invention, discovery, and improvement, were very limited; but by the introduction of each of these, they were greatly multiplied. When writing was invented, any important observation, likely to lead to a discovery, had at least a chance of being written down, and consequently, a better chance of never being forgotten; and of being seen, and reflected upon, by a much greater number of persons; and thereby the chances of a valuable hint being caught, proportionably augmented. By this means the observation of a single individual might lead to an important invention, years, and even centuries after he was dead. In one word, by means of writing, the seeds of invention were more permanently preserved, and more widely sown. And yet, for the three thousand years during which printing remained undiscovered after writing was in use, it was only a small portion of the people who could write, or read writing; and consequently the field of invention, though much extended, still continued very limited. At length printing came. It gave ten thousand copies of any written matter, quite as cheaply as ten were given before; and consequently a thousand minds were brought into the field where there was but one before. This was a great *gain*; and history shows a great *change* corresponding to it, in point of time. I will venture to consider *it*, the true termination of that period called "the dark ages." Discoveries, inventions, and improvements followed rapidly, and have been increasing their rapidity ever since. The effects could not come, all at once. It required time to bring them out; and they are still coming. The *capacity* to read, could not be multiplied as fast as the *means* of reading. Spelling-books just began to go into the hands of the children; but the teachers were not very numerous, or very competent; so that it is safe to infer they did not advance so speedily as they do now-a-days. It is very probable—almost certain—that the great mass of men, at that time, were utterly unconscious, that their *conditions*, or their *minds* were capable of improvement. They not only looked upon the educated few as superior beings; but they supposed themselves to be naturally incapable of rising to equality. To emancipate the mind from this false and under estimate of itself, is the great task which printing came into the world to perform. It is difficult for us, *now* and *here*, to conceive how strong this slavery of the mind was; and how long it did, of necessity, take, to break its shackles, and to get a habit of freedom of thought, established. It is, in this connection, a curious fact that a new country is most favorable—almost necessary—to the emancipation of thought, and the consequent advancement of civilization and the arts. The human family originated as is thought, somewhere in Asia, and have worked their way princip[al]ly Westward. Just now, in civilization, and the arts, the people of Asia are entirely behind those of Europe; those of the East of Europe behind those of the West of it; while we, here in America, *think* we discover, and invent, and improve, faster than any of them. *They* may think this is arrogance; but they cannot deny that Russia has called on us to show her how to build steam-boats and railroads—while in the older parts of Asia, they scarcely know that such things as S.B.s & R.R.s exist. In anciently inhabited countries, the dust of ages—a real downright old-fogyism—seems to settle upon, and smother the intellects and energies of man. It is in this view that I have mentioned the discovery of America as an event greatly favoring and facilitating useful discoveries and inventions.

Next came the Patent laws. These began in England in 1624; and, in this country, with the adoption of our constitution. Before then [these?], any man might instantly use what another had invented; so that the inventor had no special advantage from his own invention. The patent system changed this; secured to the inventor, for a limited time, the exclusive use of his invention; and thereby added the fuel of *interest* to the *fire* of genius, in the discovery and production of new and useful things.

1. Abraham Lincoln's Mechanical Mind

1. Roy P. Basler, "Lincoln as a Man of Letters," in *Lincoln for the Ages*, ed. Ralph G. Newman (New York: Doubleday, 1960), 369.

2. Benjamin P. Thomas, foreword, *Lincoln and the Tools of War*, by Robert V. Bruce (Indianapolis, IN: Bobbs-Merrill, 1956), vii.

3. Abraham Lincoln, autobiography written for John L. Scripps, June 1860, *The Collected Works of Abraham Lincoln*, ed. Roy P. Basler, with the assistance of Marion Dolores Pratt and Lloyd A. Dunlap, 9 vols. (New Brunswick, NJ: Rutgers University Press, 1953–55), 4:64; John Hanks, interview by William Herndon, Chicago, June 13, 1865, Douglas L. Wilson and Rodney O. Davis, eds., *Herndon's Informants: Letters, Interviews, and Statements about Abraham Lincoln* (Urbana: University of Illinois Press, 1998), 44; William Jayne, "Personal Reminiscences of Abraham Lincoln," address, Springfield chapter, Daughters of the American Revolution, February 12, 1907, at the Lincoln Home (privately printed, 1907), 7–8.

4. Nathaniel Grigsby to William Herndon, Gentryville, September 4, 1865, and Grigsby, interview by Herndon, September 12, 1865, and A. H. Chapman to William Herndon, September 8, 1865, and Green B. Taylor, interview by Herndon, September 16, 1865, and Anna Caroline Gentry, interview by Herndon, September 17, 1865, Wilson and Davis, *Herndon's Informants*, 94, 100–102, 114, 129, 131; William H. Herndon and Jesse W. Weik, *Herndon's Lincoln*, ed. Douglas L. Wilson and Rodney O. Davis (Urbana: Knox College Lincoln Studies Center and University of Illinois Press), 51–53.

5. William G. Greene, interview by William Herndon, May 30, 1865, Wilson and Davis, *Herndon's Informants*, 17.

6. John Hanks, interview by William Herndon, June 13, 1865, and undated interview [1865–66], Wilson and Davis, *Herndon's Informants*, 43, 457; Herndon and Weik, *Herndon's Lincoln*, 59. Lincoln's presidential secretaries, John G. Nicolay and John Hay, in their ten-volume biography of their former employer wrote of the event, "Nobody knew what to do about the disaster except 'the bow-oar,' who is described as a gigantic youth 'with his trousers rolled up some five feet,' who was wading about the boat and rigging up some undescribed contrivance by which the cargo was unloaded, the boat tilted and the water let out by boring a hole through the bottom, and everything brought safely to mooring below the dam"; *Abraham Lincoln: A History*, 10 vols. (New York: Century, 1917), 1:71.

7. John Hanks, interview by William Herndon, June 13, 1865, and undated interview (1865–66), Wilson and Davis, *Herndon's Informants*, 457; Nicolay and Hay, *Abraham Lincoln*, 1:71; Herndon and Weik, *Herndon's Lincoln*, 59.

8. Coleman Smoot to William Herndon, Petersburg, Illinois, May 7, 1866, Wilson and Davis, *Herndon's Informants*, 254; Herndon and Weik, *Herndon's Lincoln*, 59.

9. For some interesting essays on Lincoln's early education, see "Lincoln's Education" and "Young Abraham Lincoln and Log College" in M. L. Houser, *Lincoln's Education and Other Essays* (New York: Bookman, 1957), 15–71.

10. While history often wonders at the dexterity and capability of Lincoln's mental powers, he himself said he was a slow learner. His friend Joshua Speed recalled Lincoln as saying, "My mind is like a piece of steel, very hard to scratch any thing on it and almost impossible after you get it there to rub it out." Joshua Speed to William Herndon, Louisville, December 6, 1866, Wilson and Davis, *Herndon's Informants*, 499.

11. For an interesting examination of the Whig support of Taylor and of Lincoln's New England stump tour, see Reinhard H. Luthin, "Abraham Lincoln and the Massachusetts Whigs in 1848," *New England Quarterly Review* 14, no. 4 (December 1941): 619–32.

12. William Herndon originally told the story, incorrectly, that the *Globe* was the stranded boat, and Lincoln, as a passenger, helped free his own troubled vessel. In reality, as Wayne C. Temple proved in 1986, it was not the *Globe* but the *Canada* that grounded, and Lincoln was merely an observer, not a participant in its escape. *Lincoln's Connection with the Illinois & Michigan Canal, His Return from Congress in '48, and His Invention* (Springfield, IL: Illinois Bell, 1986), 35.

13. Temple, *Lincoln's Connection*, 35; Herndon and Weik, *Herndon's Lincoln*, 188; William Herndon, "Lincoln's Boat," in *The Hidden Lincoln: From the Letters and Papers of William H. Herndon*, ed. Emanuel Hertz (New York: Viking, 1938), 396–97.

14. Abraham Lincoln, 1849, "Improved Method for Lifting Vessels over Shoals," U.S. Patent 6,469, filed March 10, 1849, and issued May 22, 1849; Basler, *Collected Works*, 2:32–36; Herndon, "Lincoln's Boat," 396–97.

15. Lincoln, "Improved Method"; Basler, *Collected Works*, 2:32–36; Herndon, "Lincoln's Boat," 396–97.

16. Ralph Waldo Emerson, "The American Scholar: Phi Beta Kappa Address, Harvard, 1837," *Works of Emerson*, ed. Edward Waldo Emerson, 12 vols. (1903; repr., New York: AMS, 1968), 1:94–95.

17. For duration of time Lincoln spent working on his invention while at home from October 1, 1848 through November 26, 1848, see Earl

Schenck Miers, *Lincoln Day by Day: A Chronology, 1809–1865*, 3 vols. (Dayton, OH: Morningside, 1991), 1:320–24.

18. Jesse W. Weik, *The Real Lincoln: A Portrait* (Boston: Houghton Mifflin, 1922), 242. Variations of Herndon's recollection on this can be found in Herndon, "Lincoln's Boat," 396–97; and Herndon and Weik, *Herndon's Lincoln*, 188. Less than one month after submitting his patent application, Lincoln recommended Walter Davis, the man who aided him in making his patent model, to be a receiver of the General Land Office in Springfield, Illinois. Lincoln to Thomas Ewing, Secretary of the Home Department, Springfield, Illinois, April 7, 1849, Basler, *Collected Works*, 2:40.

19. Herndon and Weik, *Herndon's Lincoln*, 188.

20. Dennis F. Hanks, interview by Erastus Wright, Chicago, June 8, 1865, and by William Herndon, June 13, 1865, and J. W. Wartmann to William Herndon, Rockport, Indiana, July 21, 1865, and Nathaniel Grigsby to William Herndon, Gentryville, September 4, 1865, Wilson and Davis, *Herndon's Informants*, 28, 40, 79, 94.

21. John Romine, interview by William Herndon, September 14, 1865, Wilson and Davis, *Herndon's Informants*, 118; Herndon and Weik, *Herndon's Lincoln*, 40.

22. Grant Goodrich to William Herndon, Chicago, December 9, 1866, Wilson and Davis, *Herndon's Informants*, 510.

23. Henry Clay Whitney, *Life on the Circuit with Lincoln* (Caldwell, ID: Caxton, 1940), 121.

24. Herndon and Weik, *Herndon's Lincoln*, 353–54.

25. David C. Mearns, *The Lincoln Papers: The Story of the Collection*, 2 vols. (Garden City, NY: Doubleday, 1948), 1:4–5; Kenneth W. Dobyns, *The Patent Office Pony: A History of the Early Patent Office* (Fredericksburg, VA: Sergeant Kirkland's Museum and Historical Society, 1994), 150.

26. Dobyns, *Patent Office Pony*, 186–87; Mary Clemmer Ames, *Ten Years in Washington: Life and Scenes in the National Capital as a Woman Sees Them* (Hartford, CT: Worthington, 1873), 437. The patent office was 410 feet long by 275 feet wide, stretching from Seventh to Ninth and F to G streets. Dobyns, *Patent Office Pony*, 186–87; Ames, *Ten Years in Washington*, 437.

27. Ames, *Ten Years in Washington*, 438; Dobyns, *Patent Office Pony*, 185.

28. Ames, *Ten Years in Washington*, 438.

29. Dobyns, *Patent Office Pony*, 185.

30. Mearns, *Lincoln Papers*, 1:4–5.

31. Weik, *Real Lincoln*, 238–39; Robert B. Rutledge to William Herndon, Oskaloosa, Iowa, November 30, 1866, and Joseph Gillespie to William Herndon, Edwardsville, Illinois, December 8, 1866, and John T. Stuart, interview by William Herndon, December 20, 1866, Wilson

and Davis, *Herndon's Informants*, 426, 505–6, 519; "Lincoln, Miss Roby, and Astronomy," *Lincoln Lore*, no. 1349, February 14, 1955.

Henry Clay Whitney stated that one of Lincoln's favorite books was Francis Bacon's *Essays*. Perhaps part of the reason for Lincoln's multifaceted list of study topics was influenced by Bacon, who wrote of studies, "Histories make men wise; poets, witty; the mathematics, subtile; natural philosophy, deep; moral, grave; logic and rhetoric, able to contend: *Studies go to form character*." Such a reading list and description of its influence fit Lincoln well. Whitney, *Life on the Circuit*, 136; Francis Bacon, *Essays and New Atlantis*, Classics Club edition (New York: Black, 1942), 208.

32. Leonard Swett, "Mr. Lincoln's Story of His Own Life," in *Reminiscences of Abraham Lincoln by Distinguished Men of His Time*, ed. by Allen Thorndike Rice, rev. ed. (New York: Harper & Brothers, 1909), 79.

33. Ibid., 458; David Turnham, interview by William Herndon, September 15, 1865, Wilson and Davis, *Herndon's Informants*, 121. For an interesting monograph on the subject of Lincoln's mathematical education while a boy in Indiana, see M. L. Houser, *Young Abraham Lincoln: Mathematician* (Peoria, IL: Schriver, 1943).

34. Abraham Lincoln, autobiography written for John L. Scripps, June 1860, Basler, *Collected Works*, 4:65; Nicolay and Hay, *Abraham Lincoln*, 1:115–17; Isaac Arnold, Lincoln's friend and colleague, later wrote that Lincoln was a "skillful and accurate surveyor," so accurate that "he was much sought after to survey, fix and mark the boundary of farms, and to plot and lay off new towns and villages." Isaac N. Arnold, *The Life of Abraham Lincoln* (1884; repr., Lincoln: University of Nebraska Press, Bison Books, 1994), 41.

35. Lincoln clearly took great pride in this accomplishment, going so far as to mention it in his 1860 autobiographical sketch. Abraham Lincoln, autobiography written for John L. Scripps, June 1860, Basler, *Collected Works*, 4:62; William Herndon to Jesse Weik, Springfield, 11 February 1887, Hertz, *Hidden Lincoln*, 172. Robert T. Lincoln remembered from his early boyhood seeing his father study Euclid. Robert Lincoln to Isaac Markens, Manchester, Vermont, November 4, 1917, folder 5, Robert Todd Lincoln Papers, Chicago History Museum.

36. V. H., "Abraham Lincoln: His Office, His House, and His Tomb, as They Are: Interesting Reminiscences," *Cincinnati Commercial*, July 25, 1867, 2; also reprinted in Wayne C. Temple, "Herndon on Lincoln: An Unknown Interview with a List of Books in the Lincoln & Herndon Law Office," *Journal of the Illinois State Historical Society* 98, no. 1–2 (spring–summer 2005): 34–50. For lists of other books Lincoln read, see Robert Bray, "What Abraham Lincoln Read—An Evaluative and Annotated List," *Journal of the Abraham Lincoln Association* 28, no. 2

(summer 2007): 28–81, and "Some Books That Lincoln Read" and "A List of Books That Lincoln Read" in Houser, *Lincoln's Education*, 114–36, 317–24. On Lincoln's general intellectual development, see also Allen C. Guelzo, *Abraham Lincoln: Redeemer President* (Grand Rapids, MI: Eerdmans, 1999).

37. According to Albert J. Beveridge, the *Annual of Science* was actually the *Annual of Scientific Discovery*, edited by David Ames Wells, 1850–71. *Abraham Lincoln, 1809–1858*, 4 vols. (Cambridge, MA: Riversides, 1928), 2:221–25.

38. William Herndon to Jesse Weik, Springfield, December 16, 1885, Hertz, *Hidden Lincoln*, 113; Weik, *Real Lincoln*, 239.

39. Abraham Lincoln, address, Wisconsin State Agricultural Society, Milwaukee, Wisconsin, September 30, 1859, in Basler, *Collected Works*, 3:476; 479; 480. Prior to his speech at the Wisconsin State Agricultural Society, Lincoln expounded on the benefits of free labor in September 17, 1859, speeches at Dayton and Cincinnati, Ohio. See Basler, *Collected Works*, 3:436–62, and "Fragment on Free Labor," Basler, *Collected Works*, 3:462–63.

40. Basler, *Collected Works*, 3:480. The parenthetical, [how], was in two newspaper reports of the speech but not in another.

41. Abraham Lincoln, Communication to the People of Sangamo County, March 9, 1832, Basler, *Collected Works*, 1:5; 6.

42. Joshua Speed, interview by William Herndon, 1865–66, Wilson and Davis, *Herndon's Informants*, 476. DeWitt Clinton was governor of New York State from 1817 to 1823 and 1825 to 1828, among his many other local and national political positions. He was ardently in favor of improving New York's interior development and was largely responsible for the creation of the Erie Canal.

43. Abraham Lincoln, "Speech in United States House of Representatives on Internal Improvements," in Basler, *Collected Works*, 1:480–90.

44. Abraham Lincoln, "Annual Messages to Congress, December 1, 1862, December 8, 1863, and December 6, 1864," in Basler, *Collected Works*, 5:526, 7:48, 8:146. During his presidency, Lincoln advocated and signed into law the Homestead Act (free dispersal of public lands out west subject to improvement and five years of residence), the first Morill Land-Grant Act (donating public lands to states and territories that may provide colleges for the benefit of agriculture and mechanic arts), four Pacific Railroad Acts (to construct a transcontinental railroad and telegraph line), and the creation of the Department of Agriculture.

45. Gaius Paddock, "Is the Sangamon River Navigable?" *Journal of the Illinois State Historical Society* 13, no. 1 (April 1920): 49; Hamilton Thornton, "This St. Louisan Recalls Lincoln as a Spinner of Yarns in a Town Grocery," *St. Louis Globe Democrat*, n.d., Reminiscences of Springfield

Area Residents folder, Lincoln Collection, Abraham Lincoln Presidential Library.

46. Paddock, "Is the Sangamon River Navigable?" 48–50.

47. Zenas C. Robbins, interview by Ida Tarbell, n.d., in Ida Tarbell, *The Life of Abraham Lincoln*, 4 vols. (New York: Lincoln History Society, 1908), 2:21–22. Historian George Alfred Townsend also spoke with Robbins and likewise related, "Mr. Lincoln came into Mr. Robbins' office at the corner of F and Seventh Streets, with the model under his arm." *Washington, Outside and Inside: A Picture and a Narrative of the Origin, Growth, Excellences, Abuses, Beauties, and Personages of Our Governing City* (Hartford, CT: Betts, 1873), 716. What is interesting, as well as disappointing, is that Ida Tarbell's interview notes with Robbins are not among the numerous other interview manuscripts located in the contents of her papers in the Ida M. Tarbell Collection or in the Lincoln Collection at Allegheny College, Meadville, Pennsylvania. Jane Westenfeld, reference librarian, Pelletier Library, Allegheny College, e-mail to the author, November 9, 2006.

48. Benjamin Perley Poore, "Lincoln and the Newspaper Correspondents," in Rice, *Reminiscences of Abraham Lincoln*, 332; Temple, *Lincoln's Connection*, 62–63; "Lincoln and Webster," *Lincoln Lore*, no. 889, April 22, 1946.

49. Daniel Webster to Abraham Lincoln, February 28 [1849], Charles M. Wiltse, ed., *The Papers of Daniel Webster*, series 1: Correspondence, 7 vols. (Hanover, NH: University Press of New England, 1984), 6:38. Wiltse inferred in footnote 3 that this letter referred to Lincoln's patent. Thomas Ewbank was appointed commissioner of patents in May 1849.

50. Donald W. Riddle, *Congressman Abraham Lincoln* (Urbana: University of Illinois Press, 1957), 137–38; "A. Lincoln Manner of Buoying Vessels over Shoals," *Lincoln Lore*, no. 1439, January 1958; Temple, *Lincoln's Connection*, 62–63; "Lincoln and Webster," *Lincoln Lore*, no. 889, 22 April 1946; Wiltse, *Papers of Daniel Webster*, 6:38n3.

51. Temple, *Lincoln's Connection*, 62–63. Interestingly, Webster did not support Lincoln just two months later in the latter's bid to be appointed commissioner of the General Land Office. Webster seems even to have been instrumental in gaining the position for his friend Justin Butterfield, a Chicago attorney and Lincoln's main competitor for the job (Josiah M. Lucas to Abraham Lincoln, April 15, 1849, series 1, reel 1, frame 247, Abraham Lincoln Papers, Library of Congress; Elizabeth Sawyer [daughter of Justin Butterfield] to Jesse Weik, Chicago, October 12, 1888, in Herndon and Weik, *Herndon's Lincoln*, 190n; Richard Nelson Current, "Lincoln and Daniel Webster," *Journal of the Illinois State Historical Society* 48, no. 3 (autumn 1955): 312. For the full narrative of Lincoln's attempt to be General Land Office commissioner—and

the subsequent offer to him of the governorship of the Oregon Territory—see Nicolay and Hay, *Abraham Lincoln*, 1:292–97, or the various letters on the subject spanning from February 20 to July 22, 1849, in Basler, *Collected Works*, 2:28–60.

52. Harry Goldsmith, "Abraham Lincoln, Invention and Patents," *Journal of the Patent Office Society* 20, no. 1 (January 1938): 17.

53. Zenas C. Robbins to Abraham Lincoln, Washington, DC, April 13, 1849, series 1, reel 1, frame 245, Abraham Lincoln Papers, Library of Congress.

54. Abraham Lincoln, "Improved Method of Lifting Vessels over Shoals," U.S. Patent 6,469, filed March 10, 1849, and issued May 22, 1849, U.S. Patent Office, *Report of the Commissioner of Patents, for the Year 1849*, 31st Congress, 1st Session, Ex. Doc. no. 20 (Washington, DC: Office of Printers to House of Representatives, 1850), 265; Basler, *Collected Works*, 2:32–36; "List of Patents Issued from the United States Patent Office," *Scientific American*, June 2, 1849, 294.

55. Goldsmith, "Abraham Lincoln," 17.

56. William Herndon, "Lincoln's Boat," in Hertz, *Hidden Lincoln*, 396–97.

57. Paddock, "Is the Sangamon River Navigable?" 50.

58. Mark E. Neely, *The Abraham Lincoln Encyclopedia* (New York: McGraw-Hill, 1982), 162.

59. B. G. Foster, *Abraham Lincoln, Inventor* (Foster, 1928), 8; Temple, *Lincoln's Connection*, 70.

60. Abraham Lincoln to Benjamin Kellogg, Washington, April 21, 1848, and Abraham Lincoln to Amos Williams, Washington, December 8, 1848, Basler, *Collected Works*, 1:466–67, 2:14–15.

61. Martha L. Benner and Cullom Davis, eds., *The Law Practice of Abraham Lincoln: Complete Documentary Edition*, DVD-ROM (Urbana: University of Illinois Press, 2000).

62. Grant Goodrich to William Herndon, Chicago, December 9, 1866, Wilson and Davis, *Herndon's Informants*, 509–10; Herndon and Weik, *Herndon's Lincoln*, 205–6.

63. Ibid.

64. *Hildreth v. Turner*, 17 Ill. 184 (1855), and *Myers et al. v. William Turner*, 17 Ill. 184 (1855); Benner and Davis, *Law Practice*.

65. Weik, *Real Lincoln*, 158–59.

66. *Rugg v. Haines*, in Daniel W. Stowell, ed., with the assistance of Susan Krause, John A. Lupton, Stacy Pratt McDermott, Christopher A. Schnell, and Dennis E. Suttles, *The Papers of Abraham Lincoln: Legal Documents and Cases*, 4 vols. (Charlottesville: University of Virginia Press, 2008), 3:248–85. I am indebted to Daniel W. Stowell, director and editor of the Papers of Abraham Lincoln, for directing me to this case.

67. Robert R. Hitt, journal, c. March 1858, box 42, Robert R. Hitt Papers, Library of Congress.

68. Charles S. Zane, "Lincoln as I Knew Him," *Sunset Magazine* 29 (October 1912): 430–38, typescript in Reminiscences folder 1, Lincoln Collection, Abraham Lincoln Presidential Library.

69. *McCormick v. Manny et al.*, 15 F Cas. 1314 (1856). For a full legal explanation of the case and its arguments, see, "Recent American Decisions: In the Circuit Court of the United States, Northern District of Illinois, July term, 1855: *Cyrus H. McCormick v. John H. Manny, et al*," *American Law Register* 4, no. 5 (March 1856): 277–93. For the story of Lincoln's role in the case, see Robert Henry Parkinson, "The Patent Case That Lifted Lincoln into a Presidential Candidate," *Abraham Lincoln Quarterly* 4, no. 3 (September 1946): 105–22.

70. Abraham Lincoln to Peter H. Watson, Springfield, July 23, 1855, Basler, *Collected Works*, 2:314–15.

71. Herndon and Weik, *Herndon's Lincoln*, 219–20; Benjamin P. Thomas and Harold M. Hyman, *Stanton: The Life and Times of Lincoln's Secretary of War* (New York: Knopf, 1962), 63–66.

72. Ralph Emerson, *Personal Recollections of Abraham Lincoln by Mr. and Mrs. Ralph Emerson of Rockford, Illinois* (Rockford, IL: n.p., 1909), 5–9. See also Parkinson, "The Patent Case That Lifted Lincoln into a Presidential Candidate," 121–22.

73. Benner and Davis, *Law Practice*; Goldsmith, "Abraham Lincoln," 31.

74. Lincoln's lecture was printed in two parts in the *Collected Works of Abraham Lincoln*, as "First Lecture on Discoveries and Inventions" and "Second Lecture on Discoveries and Inventions." Because two manuscripts were found, it was assumed Lincoln wrote two versions, but Wayne C. Temple has offered convincing evidence that these two pieces were parts of the same speech. Lincoln spoke in Bloomington, Illinois, on April 6, 1858; in Jacksonville, Illinois, on February 4, 1859; in Springfield, Illinois, on February 21; in Decatur, Illinois, sometime in March; in Bloomington again on April 8, 1859; at Pontiac, Illinois, January 27, 1860; and at Springfield on April 26, 1860. "First Lecture on Discoveries and Inventions," and "Second Lecture on Discoveries and Inventions," Basler, *Collected Works*, 2:437–42 and 3:356–63; Wayne C. Temple, "Lincoln the Lecturer, Part I," *Lincoln Herald* 101, no. 3 (fall 1999): 94–110; Wayne C. Temple, "Lincoln the Lecturer, Part II," *Lincoln Herald* 101, no. 4 (winter 1999): 146–63. For an interesting critical literary analysis of Lincoln's lecture, see John Channing Briggs, *Lincoln's Speeches Reconsidered* (Baltimore: Johns Hopkins University Press, 2005), 184–220.

75. Whether this was really his motivation, Lincoln's pecuniary difficulties were true. Abraham Lincoln to Norman B. Judd, Springfield, November 16, 1858, to Daniel Rohrer, Springfield, August 19, 1859, and to

Hawkins Taylor, Springfield, September 6, 1859, Basler, *Collected Works*, 3:337, 397, 399–400.

76. Whitney, *Life on the Circuit*, 209.

77. Noah Brooks, *Washington in Lincoln's Time*, ed. Herbert Mitgang (New York: Rinehart, 1958), 269.

78. Abraham Lincoln, "First Lecture on Discoveries and Inventions," Basler, *Collected Works*, 2:437.

79. Ibid., 2:437–42.

80. Abraham Lincoln, "Second Lecture on Discoveries and Inventions," Basler, *Collected Works*, 3:361.

81. "The Congress shall have power to . . . promote the progress of science and useful arts, by securing for limited times to authors and inventors the exclusive right to their respective writings and discoveries." U.S. Constitution, art. 1, § 8, cl. 8.

82. Abraham Lincoln, "Second Lecture on Discoveries and Inventions," Basler, *Collected Works*, 3:363.

83. *Illinois State Journal*, February 21, 1859, 3; Weik, *Real Lincoln*, 243. For the most thorough examination of Lincoln's lecture, its deliveries and audience reactions, see Temple, "Lincoln the Lecturer," parts 1 and 2.

84. William Herndon to Jesse Weik, Springfield, February 21, 1891, Hertz, *Hidden Lincoln*, 262.

85. Jayne also later said the crowd was so small that Lincoln took no fee for speaking. "Well, boys," Lincoln supposedly told the Phi Alpha Society committee that invited him, "be hopeful; pay me my railroad fare and fifty cents for my supper at the hotel and we'll call it square." *Personal Reminiscences of the Martyred President Abraham Lincoln* (Chicago: Grand Army Hall & Memorial Association, 1908), 24–25, and "Personal Reminiscences of Abraham Lincoln," 7–8; Jesse Weik also told this story based on his personal interview with Jayne. Weik, *Real Lincoln*, 243.

86. J. H. Burnham to his father, Bloomington, Illinois, May 19, 1860, quoted in *Concerning Mr. Lincoln*, ed. Harry Pratt (Springfield, IL: Abraham Lincoln Association, 1944), 22.

87. Whitney, *Life on the Circuit*, 436.

88. Augustus William Cowan to Mary P. Christian, January 28, 1860, quoted in Pratt, *Concerning Mr. Lincoln*, 21.

89. Abraham Lincoln to William M. Morris, Springfield, March 28, 1859, and to Thomas J. Pickett, Springfield, April 16, 1859, Basler, *Collected Works*, 3:374, 377.

90. William Herndon to Jesse Weik, Springfield, November 17, 1885, Hertz, *Hidden Lincoln*, 104.

91. Abraham Lincoln to F. C. Herbruger, April 7, 1860, and to John M. Carson, April 7, 1860, Basler, *Collected Works*, 4:39, 40; Brooks, *Washington in Lincoln's Time*, 269.

92. "The President Elect's Mode of Buoying Vessels," *Scientific American*, December 1, 1860, 356; see also 362.

93. "President Lincoln's Model," *Boston Daily Advertiser*, May 15, 1865, 2; "President Lincoln as an Inventor," *Scientific American*, May 27, 1865, 340.

94. Ames, *Ten Years in Washington*, 443; Dobyns, *Patent Office Pony*, 188.

95. "A Presidential Patent," *Harper's Weekly* 5, April 6, 1861, 210.

96. U.S. Congress, *Congressional Globe*, 37th Cong., 3rd Sess. 1863, 3:1530; Miers, *Lincoln Day by Day*, 3:171–72. According to the National Academy of Sciences (NAS) Web site, the organization is "an honorific society of distinguished scholars engaged in scientific and engineering research, dedicated to the furtherance of science and technology and to their use for the general welfare." Its Act of Incorporation, Senate Bill S. 555, 37th Cong. (1863), stated the society would serve to "investigate, examine, experiment, and report upon any subject of science or art" whenever called upon to do so by any department of the government. Lincoln signed the NAS into being on March 3, 1863. "About the NAS," National Academy of Sciences Web site, http://www.nasonline.org/site/PageServer?pagename=ABOUT_main_page.

97. "War and Inventions," *Scientific American*, May 25, 1861, 329.

98. John Hay, "Life in the White House in the Time of Lincoln," in *Addresses of John Hay* (New York: Century, 1907), 327–28. Originally this was published in *Century Magazine*, November 1890, 319–41.

99. Ibid.

100. Abraham Lincoln to Richard Delafield, Office of Chief of Engineers, July 28, 1864, and to Montgomery C. Meigs, Quarter Master General, January 12, 1865, Basler, *Collected Works*, 7:468, 8:213; Bruce, *Lincoln and the Tools of War*; Mark E. Neely, "'. . . One of the Little Breech-loading Cannons I Got of Hon. Eli Thayer,'" *Lincoln Lore*, no. 1665 (November 1976): 1–4.

101. Abraham Lincoln, Memorandum Concerning Harbor Defenses, April 4, 1863, Basler, *Collected Works*, 6:163.

102. Madeleine Vinton Dahlgren, ed., *Memoir of John A. Dahlgren* (Boston: Osgood, 1882), 378, 379, 383, 386, 388.

103. Ibid., 383.

104. Robert J. Schneller Jr., *A Quest for Glory: A Biography of Rear Admiral John A Dahlgren* (Annapolis, MD: Naval Institute Press, 1996), 186.

105. Bruce, *Lincoln and the Tools of War*, 21; Schneller, *Quest for Glory*, 185–86.

106. Gideon Welles, diary entry, February 22, 1863, *Diary of Gideon Welles: Secretary of the Navy under Lincoln and Johnson*, 3 vols. (Boston: Houghton Mifflin, 1911), 1:239–40.

107. John A. Dahlgren, diary entry, April 28, 1863, in Dahlgren, *Memoir of John A. Dahlgren*, 390–91.

108. "President Lincoln's Model," *Boston Daily Advertiser*, May 15, 1865, 2; "President Lincoln as an Inventor—His Model at Washington," *New York Times*, May 19, 1865, 2; "President Lincoln as an Inventor," 340. Nicolay and Hay wrote in 1894 that Lincoln's model still was in the patent office as an item of public admiration and curiosity: "We have never learned that it has served any other purpose." *Abraham Lincoln*, 1:71.

109. "President Lincoln's Model."

110. "President Lincoln as an Inventor," *Scientific American*, May 27, 1865, 340.

111. Clark Moulton Smith, interview by John Nicolay, July 8, 1875, John G. Nicolay Papers, Manuscripts Division, Library of Congress, Washington, DC; also published in *An Oral History of Abraham Lincoln: John G. Nicolay's Interviews and Essays*, ed. Michael Burlingame (Carbondale: Southern Illinois University Press, 1996), 18. In 1864, a member of the New York Sanitary Commission asked President Lincoln if the committee on machinery could reproduce a model of his invention, "knowing that its high associations would make it an object of great attraction." Despite Lincoln's typical generosity towards sanitary commissions, there is no evidence that he consented to this request. Adam S. Cameron to President Abraham Lincoln, New York, March 10, 1864, series 1, reel 70, frame 31440, Abraham Lincoln Papers, Library of Congress.

112. A search of the Southern Illinois University Edwardsville and Carbondale archives, museums, and libraries failed to discover the model, as did conversations with numerous past employees of Shurtleff College, Alton, Illinois. Steve Kerber, Southern Illinois University archivist and Special Collections librarian, Lovejoy Library, Southern Illinois University Edwardsville, telephone conversations with the author, November 17 and 27, 2006.

113. Jacques Barzun, *Lincoln the Literary Genius* (Evanston, IL: Evanston, 1960), 25.

114. Basler, "Lincoln as a Man of Letters," 370.

115. Emphasis added. Abraham Lincoln, "Second Lecture on Discoveries and Inventions, Basler, *Collected Works*, 3:362.

116. In 2006, Paul Johnston, curator of maritime history at the National Museum of American History, called Lincoln's patent model "one of the half dozen or so most valuable things in our collection." Owen Edwards, "Inventive Abe," *Smithsonian*, October 2006, 32.

2. Lincoln's Lecture on Discoveries and Inventions: The Unknown Draft

1. John G. Nicolay, "Lincoln's Literary Experiments," *Century Magazine*, April 1894, 832.

2. Herndon and Weik, *Herndon's Lincoln*, 271.

3. Whitney, *Life on the Circuit*, 209.

4. The essay was titled "The Necessity, the Reality, and the Promise of the Progress of the Human Race," which Bancroft delivered before the New York Historical Society on November 20, 1854, and was published in Bancroft's 1855 book, *Literary and Historical Miscellanies* (New York: Harper and Brothers).

5. Whitney, *Life on the Circuit*, 209.

6. Ibid., 499–500.

7. Noah Brooks, *Washington in Lincoln's Time* (New York: Rinehart, 1958), 269. Lincoln's premise that nothing invented was actually new also seems to have been based on the Bible, for it echoed Solomon's decree in Ecclesiastes 1:9: "There is no new thing under the sun." This also is similar to Plato's philosophical theory of knowledge and his term *anamnesis*, which he developed in the dialogues of the *Meno* and the *Phaedo* and that Francis Bacon condensed into the definition that "all knowledge was but remembrance." Socrates believed the soul to be immortal and repeatedly incarnated and that knowledge also was immortal but forgotten at each successive reincarnation. Learning then to Socrates was recalling that which one had merely forgotten in rebirth (Bacon, *Essays and New Atlantis*, 235).

8. Address before the Young Men's Lyceum of Springfield, Illinois, January 27, 1838, and Address Delivered before the Springfield Washington Temperance Society, February 22, 1842, Eulogy on Zachary Taylor, Chicago, July 25, 1850, and Eulogy on Henry Clay, July 6, 1852, Basler, *Collected Works*, 1:108–15, 271–79; 2:83–90, 121–32.

9. Address before the Wisconsin State Agricultural Society, Milwaukee, Wisconsin, September 30, 1859, Basler, *Collected Works*, 3:471–82.

10. Fragment: Niagara Falls, September 25–30, 1848, and Fragment: Notes for a Law Lecture, July 1, 1850, Basler, *Collected Works*, 2:10–11, 81–82.

11. For more information on this cultural phenomenon, see Carl Bode, *The American Lyceum: Town Meeting of the Mind* (New York: Oxford University Press, 1956).

12. "Mr. Lincoln's Lecture," *Bloomington (Illinois) Daily Pantagraph*, April 5, 7, 9, 1858, 3.

13. Ibid., April 9, 1858, 3.

14. *Jacksonville (Illinois) Sentinel*, February 11, 1859, 2, and *Illinois State Journal*, February 14, 1859, 3, quoted in Wayne C. Temple, "Lincoln the Lecturer, Part I," *Lincoln Herald* 101, no. 3 (fall 1999): 109; Jayne, *Personal Reminiscences*, 24–25; Jayne, *Personal Reminiscences*, 7–8; Jesse Weik also told this story based on his personal interview with Jayne (*Real Lincoln*, 243); *Illinois State Journal*, February 21, 1859, 3; Samuel H. Melvin, affidavit, "Memorandum of Certain Facts for Information

of Those Who Follow After," in *Discoveries and Inventions: A Lecture by Abraham Lincoln Delivered in 1860*, ed. John Howell (San Francisco: Howell, 1915), 17; Herndon and Weik, *Herndon's Lincoln*, 271.

15. *Daily Pantagraph*, April 6 and 9, 1859, 3, 3; J. H. Burnham to his father, Bloomington, Illinois, May 19, 1860, in Pratt, *Concerning Mr. Lincoln*, 22.

16. Augustus William Cowan to Mary P. Christian, January 28, 1860, in Pratt, *Concerning Mr. Lincoln*, 21.

17. *Illinois State Journal*, April 25 and 26, 1860, 3, 3; John Nicolay to Robert Lincoln, Washington, December 16, 1890, box 5, Nicolay Papers, Library of Congress; Melvin affidavit, in Howell, *Discoveries and Inventions*, 17.

18. *Illinois State Journal*, April 28, 1860, 3.

19. Abraham Lincoln to William M. Morris, Springfield, March 28, 1859, Abraham Lincoln to Thomas J. Pickett, Springfield, April 16, 1859, Abraham Lincoln to John M. Carson, Springfield, April 7, 1860, Abraham Lincoln to F. C. Herbruger, Springfield, April 7, 1860, in Basler, *Collected Works*, 3:374, 377, and 4:39, 40; "Mr. Lincoln, Having Been Invited to Lecture before a Literary Association in Philadelphia, Declined for Reasons Stated in His Note," *Lowell (Massachusetts) Daily Citizen and News*, October 24, 1860, 1.

20. For a detailed examination of this aspect of Lincoln's interest, see Bruce, *Lincoln and the Tools of War*.

21. Whitney, *Life on the Circuit*, 499; Brooks, *Washington in Lincoln's Time*, 269.

22. Basler, *Collected Works*, 3:356n1.

23. Temple, "Lincoln the Lecturer, Part I," 97–98, 100.

24. Dr. Melvin actually had a long and intimate history with the Lincolns. He became Lincoln's pharmacist, and the two men often played checkers in Melvin's store; Mary Lincoln and Sarah Melvin were friends; the Melvins named their daughter after Mary Lincoln; both families attended the First Presbyterian Church; and President Lincoln offered Dr. Melvin a government position. For a full history of the Lincoln-Melvin friendship, see Wayne C. Temple, *Abraham Lincoln: From Skeptic to Prophet* (Mahomet, IL: Mayhaven, 1995), 97–101.

25. Melvin, affidavit, in Howell, ed., *Discoveries and Inventions*, 15–17. Apparently, whenever Mrs. Grimsley was asked for a Lincoln souvenir, she gave away a paper from the satchel. This, combined with an errant servant's burning of the rest of the contents thinking they were refuse, eventually left the bag empty. For more on the story of the carpetbag, see Justin G. Turner, "Lincolniana: The Grimsley Trunk," *Journal of the Illinois State Historical Society* 66, no. 4 (winter 1973): 456, and Carl Sandburg, *Lincoln Collector: The Story of Oliver R. Barrett's Great Private Collection* (New York: Harcourt, Brace, 1949), 75–80.

26. Temple, "Lincoln the Lecturer, Part I," 100.

27. Charles Gunther was a Chicago candymaker who began displaying historic curios in his downtown factory in the 1880s. He eventually created a huge Civil War museum housed in the notorious Confederate prisoner-of-war camp Libby Prison, which he purchased from Richmond, Virginia, dismantled, and shipped to Chicago. By the turn of the century, Gunther owned one of the largest collections of Lincoln artifacts in America. Oliver R. Barrett was a prominent Chicago attorney and antiquarian who began collecting Lincolniana while a boy in the 1880s. By the early twentieth century, Barrett was one of the foremost Lincoln collectors in America. "The Bloody Evidence—The Lincoln Assassination Artifacts—The Story of Libby Prison—Charles Gunther's Civil War Museum," Chicago History Museum Web site, http://chicagohistory.org/wetwithblood/bloody /index.htm; "Relics of Lincoln in Chicago," *Chicago Tribune*, February 10, 1895, 27; "Libby Prison," *Chicago Herald*, September 21, 1889, 5; "C. F. Gunther Secures More Relics," *Chicago Tribune*, December 2, 1892, 6; Melvin, affidavit, Howell, *Discoveries and Inventions*, 17; Basler, *Collected Works*, 2:437n1; Temple, "Lincoln the Lecturer, Part I," 100. For the story of Barrett and his Lincoln collection, see Sandburg, *Lincoln Collector*; for the relationship between Barrett and Gunther, see Sandburg, *Lincoln Collector*, 15–18. The Meisei University in Tokyo, Japan, now has the Barrett copy, while the Melvin copy resides in Morris Library, Southern Illinois University, Carbondale.

28. Temple, "Lincoln the Lecturer, Part I," 100.

29. Ibid., 102; Briggs, *Lincoln's Speeches Reconsidered*, 191.

30. "Mr. Lincoln's Lecture," *Bloomington (Illinois) Daily Pantagraph*, April 9, 1858, 3.

31. Nicolay, "Lincoln's Literary Experiments," 832.

32. Herndon and Weik, *Herndon's Lincoln*, 271.

33. Ward H. Lamon, *The Life of Abraham Lincoln* (1872; repr., Lincoln: University of Nebraska Press, Bison Books, 1999), 421.

34. For interesting examinations of Lincoln's oratorical reluctance, see Waldo W. Braden, "'Kindly Let Me Be Silent': A Reluctant Lincoln," *Lincoln Herald* 86, no. 4 (1984): 195–202, and Harold Holzer, "I Should Not Say Any Foolish Things," *Civil War Times* 34 (November/December 1995): 22, 106–15.

35. Robert Lincoln to F. J. Child, Washington, April 27, 1865, Robert Todd Lincoln Collection, Phillips Exeter Academy; Robert Lincoln to James Parton, Washington, May 10, 1865, Robert Todd Lincoln Family Papers, Library of Congress; Noah Brooks, "The Lincoln Family," letter from Washington, May 17, 1865, to the *Sacramento Daily Union*, published June 14, 1865, funeral reminiscences folder, Lincoln Collection, Abraham Lincoln Presidential Library.

36. The Robert Todd Lincoln Collection of the Papers of Abraham Lincoln was formally donated to the United States of America "to be deposited in the Library of Congress for the benefit of all the People" on January 23, 1923, but not opened to the public until 1947, due to the stipulation that the papers were not to be opened until twenty-one years after Robert's death. "Deed of Gift of Manuscripts and Private Papers of President Lincoln by His Son, Robert Todd Lincoln," January 23, 1923, and St. George L. Sioussat to David C. Mearns, internal Library of Congress memorandum, April 1, 1947, and David C. Mearns to the Librarian of Congress, "Property Rights, Lincoln Manuscripts and the Seward Heirs," July 17, 1951, David C. Mearns Papers, Manuscripts Division, Library of Congress. Robert Lincoln deed of gift to the Library of Congress, January 23, 1923, also in Robert Todd Lincoln Family Papers, Library of Congress. For the complete story of the history of the Lincoln papers, see Mearns, *Lincoln Papers*.

37. Nicolay and Hay's biography was serialized in forty excerpts in *Century Magazine* between 1886 and 1890 before the final book publication—by the Century Company—in 1890. For interesting histories of Nicolay and Hay's creation of their biography, see Michael Burlingame, "Nicolay and Hay: Court Historians," *Journal of the Abraham Lincoln Association* 19, no. 1 (winter 1998): 1–20, and Michael Burlingame, *Abraham Lincoln: The Observations of John G. Nicolay and John Hay* (Carbondale: Southern Illinois University Press, 2007).

   Robert Lincoln specifically requested that upon the completion of *Abraham Lincoln: A History*, that Nicolay and Hay "supplement it by collecting, editing, and publishing the speeches, letters, state papers and miscellaneous writings of my father" (Robert Lincoln to John Nicolay, May 30, 1893, box 5, Nicolay Papers, Library of Congress). See also Robert Lincoln to G. P. Putnam's Sons, December 28, 1885, vol. 3, microfilm reel 5, 791–92, Robert Todd Lincoln Letterpress Books, Abraham Lincoln Presidential Library, and Robert Lincoln to Thomas Ewing Jr., May 24, 1907, Robert Todd Lincoln Papers, Lincoln Collection, Abraham Lincoln Presidential Library.

38. Robert Lincoln to John Nicolay, October 27, 1887, box 4, Nicolay Papers, Library of Congress.

39. Ibid., December 18, 1887.

40. Ibid.

41. Robert Lincoln to John Nicolay, December 12, 1890, box 5, Nicolay Papers, Library of Congress, and vol. 13, microfilm reel 19, 131–33, Robert Todd Lincoln Letterpress Books, Abraham Lincoln Presidential Lincoln. Emphasis added.

42. John Nicolay to Robert Lincoln, Washington, January 1, 1888, box 5, Nicolay Papers, Library of Congress; Robert Lincoln to Katherine

Arnold, Chicago, May 3, 1888, folder 1, Robert Todd Lincoln Papers, Chicago History Museum. Robert's letter to Katherine Arnold was written at Nicolay's behest.

43. Katherine D. Arnold to Mary Harlan Lincoln, May 5, 1889, box 5, Nicolay Papers, Library of Congress.

44. Robert Lincoln to John Nicolay, May 8, 1889, box 5, Nicolay Papers, Library of Congress.

45. Ibid., December 6, 1890.

46. Ibid., December 12, 1890, and vol. 13, microfilm reel 19, 131–33, Robert Todd Lincoln Letterpress Books, Abraham Lincoln Presidential Library.

47. Nicolay, "Lincoln's Literary Experiments," 828–32; John G. Nicolay and John Hay, *Abraham Lincoln: Collected Works*, 2 vols. (New York: Century, 1894), 1:522–28.

48. Robert Lincoln to John Nicolay, December 12, 1890, box 5, Nicolay Papers, Library of Congress, and vol. 13, microfilm reel 19, 131–33, Robert Todd Lincoln Letterpress Books, Abraham Lincoln Presidential Library.

49. John Nicolay to Robert Lincoln, Washington, December 16, 1890, box 5, Nicolay Papers, Library of Congress.

50. Nicolay, "Lincoln's Literary Experiments," 831.

51. Eugene F. Miller, "Democratic Statecraft and Technological Advance: Abraham Lincoln's Reflections on 'Discoveries and Inventions,'" *Review of Politics* 63, no. 3 (summer 2001): 487.

52. Herndon and Weik, *Herndon's Lincoln*, 271. Ward Hill Lamon, who used Herndon's materials for his own Lincoln book, echoed this sentiment, nearly verbatim, which makes one wonder at the originality of its sentiment (*Life of Abraham Lincoln*, 421).

53. Roy P. Basler, *A Touchstone for Greatness: Essays, Addresses, and Occasional Pieces about Abraham Lincoln*, Contributions in American Studies, vol. 4 (Westport, CT: Greenwood Press, 1973), 82.

54. Garry Wills, *Lincoln at Gettysburg: The Words That Remade America* (New York: Simon and Schuster, 1992), 83.

55. Miller, "Democratic Statecraft and Technological Advance," 487–88.

56. Briggs, *Lincoln's Speeches Reconsidered*, 194–96.

Appendix 2: Lincoln's First and Second Lectures on Discoveries and Inventions

1. In 1865, Dr. Samuel H. Melvin, at the time a resident of Springfield, received the manuscript along with the manuscript of the second lecture on the same subject . . . from "aunt Lizzie" Grimsley (widow of Harrison J. Grimsley and daughter of Dr. John Todd), from the collection of papers which Lincoln had left with her before departing from Springfield in 1861. The manuscript of the second lecture was sold by

Dr. Melvin to Charles Gunther, Chicago, Illinois; the first was kept in his own possession. This first lecture was delivered at Bloomington before the Young Men's Association on April 6, 1858, and was reported in the *Bloomington Pantagraph*, April 9, 1858, sufficiently to establish the precedence of this version over that of the second lecture as revised and delivered on February 11, 1859.

2. Lincoln deletes "examples," inserts "patterns," and deletes the following sentence, which stood first in the next paragraph: "Beavers, and musk-rats, build houses, but they build no better ones *now*, than they did five thousand years ago. Ants, and honey-bees, lay up their winter stocks of provisions; but they do so, no wise better, or less laboriously, than they did at the dawn of creation."

3. The following passage has been deleted by Lincoln at this point: "But let us imagine, for a moment, that all the wheels are locked forever; and we shall at once conclude that the world is num[b]ed. A common jumper, made of hickory poles, with fifty cents worth of labor, would then be worth more than the President's carriage, and even the largest train of railroad cars in existence. Indeed the railroad itself would be utterly worthless. That wagon-load of wheat which was to have gone to the river to-morrow, can not go; and the barrel of salt which was to have been brought by the return trip, can not come. Aunt Lizzie's pleasure trip to New York, Boston, and Niagara Falls, is entirely '*done for*[.]' More particular allusion will hereafter be made to the wheel & axle."

4. The manuscript ends abruptly at the top of a page. Probably there was more to the lecture which Lincoln utilized in his revised version.

5. Lincoln's first lecture on Discoveries and Inventions was written at least by April 6, 1858 . . . , on which date he delivered it before the Young Men's Association of Bloomington, Illinois. Completely rewritten for delivery before the Phi Alpha Society of Illinois College at Jacksonville on February 11, 1859 (*Illinois State Journal*, February 14, 1859), the lecture was repeated a few days later in Decatur, and again in Springfield on February 21 before the Springfield Library Association at Concert Hall (*ibid.*, February 21). Further invitations to lecture were turned down because of pressure of business (letters to W. M. Morris, March 28, and T. J. Pickett, April 16 . . .). The second manuscript, like the first, was preserved in the satchel of documents that Lincoln left with Elizabeth Todd Grimsley a few days before leaving for Washington in 1861. It later passed into the Gunther Collection and then into the Barrett Collection.

6. Lincoln left a blank space in which "Spain" has been pencilled by another hand.

BIBLIOGRAPHY

Archival Sources

Abraham Lincoln Presidential Library, Springfield, Illinois
    Henry Horner Lincoln Collection
    Robert Todd Lincoln Letterpress Books
Allegheny College, Meadville, Pennsylvania
    Ida M. Tarbell Collection
    The Lincoln Collection
Chicago History Museum, Chicago, Illinois
    Robert Todd Lincoln Papers
Library of Congress, Washington, DC
    Robert R. Hitt Papers
    Abraham Lincoln Papers—the papers are transcribed and annotated
        in a collaborative project of the LOC Manuscript Division and
        the Lincoln Studies Center, Knox College, Galesburg, Illinois; the
        papers also are available online at http://memory.loc.gov/ammen
        /alhtml/malhome.html
    Robert Todd Lincoln Family Papers
    David C. Mearns Papers
    John G. Nicolay Papers
Phillips Exeter Academy, Exeter, New Hampshire
    Robert Todd Lincoln Collection

Newspapers

Bloomington (Illinois) Daily Pantagraph
Boston Daily Advertiser
Chicago Herald
Chicago Tribune
Cincinnati Commercial
Illinois State Journal
Lowell (Massachusetts) Daily Citizen and News
New York Times
St. Louis Globe Democrat

Books and Articles

"Abraham Lincoln an Inventor, Patent Records Reveal." *Popular Mechanics Magazine*, March 1924, 360–63.
"A. Lincoln Manner of Buoying Vessels over Shoals." *Lincoln Lore*, no. 1439, January 1958.

Ames, Mary Clemmer. *Ten Years in Washington: Life and Scenes in the National Capital as a Woman Sees Them.* Hartford, CT: Worthington, 1873.

Arnold, Isaac N. *The Life of Abraham Lincoln.* 1884. Reprint, Lincoln: University of Nebraska Press, Bison Books, 1994.

Bacon, Francis. *Essays and New Atlantis.* Classics Club edition. New York: Black, 1942.

Barzun, Jacques. *Lincoln the Literary Genius.* Evanston, IL: Evanston, 1960.

Basler, Roy P., ed. *The Collected Works of Abraham Lincoln.* With the assistance of Marion Dolores Pratt and Lloyd A. Dunlap. 9 vols. New Brunswick, NJ: Rutgers University Press, 1953–55.

———. "Lincoln as a Man of Letters." In *Lincoln for the Ages,* edited by Ralph G. Newman, 367–71. New York: Doubleday, 1960.

———. *A Touchstone for Greatness: Essays, Addresses, and Occasional Pieces about Abraham Lincoln.* Contributions in American Studies 4. Westport, CT: Greenwood, 1973.

Benner, Martha L., and Cullom Davis, eds. *The Law Practice of Abraham Lincoln: Complete Documentary Edition.* DVD. Urbana: University of Illinois Press, 2000.

Beveridge, Albert J. *Abraham Lincoln, 1809–1858.* 4 vols. Standard library edition. Cambridge, MA: Riverside, 1928.

Bode, Carl. *The American Lyceum: Town Meeting of the Mind.* New York: Oxford University Press, 1956.

Braden, Waldo W. "'Kindly Let Me Be Silent': A Reluctant Lincoln." *Lincoln Herald* 86, no. 4 (1984): 195–202.

Bray, Robert. "What Abraham Lincoln Read—An Evaluative and Annotated List." *Journal of the Abraham Lincoln Association* 28, no. 2 (Summer 2007): 28–81.

Briggs, John Channing. *Lincoln's Speeches Reconsidered.* Baltimore, MD: Johns Hopkins University Press, 2005.

Brooks, Noah. *Washington in Lincoln's Time.* Edited and with an introduction by Herbert Mitgang. New York: Rinehart, 1958.

Bruce, Robert V. *Lincoln and the Tools of War.* Indianapolis, IN: Bobbs-Merrill, 1956.

Burlingame, Michael. *Abraham Lincoln: The Observations of John G. Nicolay and John Hay.* Carbondale: Southern Illinois University Press, 2007.

———. "Nicolay and Hay: Court Historians." *Journal of the Abraham Lincoln Association* 19, no. 1 (Winter 1998): 1–20.

———, ed. *An Oral History of Abraham Lincoln: John G. Nicolay's Interviews and Essays.* Carbondale: Southern Illinois University Press, 1996.

Current, Richard Nelson. "Lincoln and Daniel Webster." *Journal of the Illinois State Historical Society* 48, no. 3 (Autumn 1955): 307–21.

Dahlgren, Madeleine Vinton, ed. *Memoir of John A. Dahlgren*. Boston: Osgood, 1882.

Dobyns, Kenneth W. *The Patent Office Pony: A History of the Early Patent Office*. Fredericksburg, VA: Sergeant Kirkland's Museum and Historical Society, 1994.

Edwards, Owen. "Inventive Abe." *Smithsonian*, October 2006, 32, 35.

Emerson, Ralph. *Personal Recollections of Abraham Lincoln by Mr. and Mrs. Ralph Emerson of Rockford, Illinois*. Rockford, IL: 1909.

Emerson, Ralph Waldo. "The American Scholar: Phi Beta Kappa Address, Harvard, 1837." In *Works of Emerson*, edited by Edward Waldo Emerson, vol. 1, 94–95. 12 vols. 1903. Reprint, New York: AMS Press, 1968.

Foster, B. G. *Abraham Lincoln, Inventor*. Foster, 1928.

Goldsmith, Harry. "Abraham Lincoln, Invention and Patents." *Journal of the Patent Office Society* 20, no. 1 (January 1938): 5–33.

Guelzo, Allen C. *Abraham Lincoln: Redeemer President*. Grand Rapids, MI: Eerdmans, 1999.

Hay, John. *Addresses of John Hay*. New York: Century, 1907.

Herndon, William H. "Lincoln's Boat." In *The Hidden Lincoln: From the Letters and Papers of William H. Herndon*, edited and compiled by Emanuel Hertz, 396–97. New York: Viking, 1938.

Herndon, William H., and Jesse W. Weik. *Herndon's Lincoln*. Edited by Douglas L. Wilson and Rodney O. Davis. Urbana: Knox College Lincoln Studies Center and University of Illinois Press, 2006.

Holzer, Harold. "I Should Not Say Any Foolish Things." *Civil War Times*, November/December 1995, 22, 106–15.

Houser, M. L. *Lincoln's Education and Other Essays*. New York: Bookman, 1957.

———. *Young Abraham Lincoln: Mathematician*. Peoria, IL: Schriver, 1943.

Howell, John, ed. *Discoveries and Inventions: A Lecture by Abraham Lincoln Delivered in 1860*. San Francisco: Howell, 1915.

Jayne, William. "Personal Reminiscences of Abraham Lincoln." Address, Springfield chapter, Daughters of the American Revolution, February 12, 1907, Lincoln Home, Springfield, Illinois. Privately printed, 1907.

———. *Personal Reminiscences of the Martyred President Abraham Lincoln*. Chicago: Grand Army Hall & Memorial Association, 1908.

Lamon, Ward H. *The Life of Abraham Lincoln*. 1872. Reprint, Lincoln: University of Nebraska Press, Bison Books, 1999.

"Lincoln and Webster." *Lincoln Lore*, no. 889, April 22, 1946.

"Lincoln, Miss Roby, and Astronomy." *Lincoln Lore*, no. 1349, February 14, 1955.

"List of Patents Issued from the United States Patent Office." *Scientific American*, June 2, 1849.

Luthin, Reinhard H. "Abraham Lincoln and the Massachusetts Whigs in 1848." *New England Quarterly Review* 14, no. 4 (December 1941): 619–32.

Mearns, David C. *The Lincoln Papers: The Story of the Collection with Selections to July 4, 1861.* 2 vols. Garden City, NY: Doubleday, 1948.

Miers, Earl Schenck. *Lincoln Day by Day: A Chronology, 1809–1865.* 3 vols. Dayton, OH: Morningside, 1991.

Miller, Eugene F. "Democratic Statecraft and Technological Advance: Abraham Lincoln's Reflections on 'Discoveries and Inventions.'" *Review of Politics* 63, no. 3 (Summer 2001): 485–515.

Neely, Mark E. *The Abraham Lincoln Encyclopedia.* New York: McGraw-Hill, 1982.

———. "'. . . One of the Little Breech-loading Cannons I Got of Hon. Eli Thayer.'" *Lincoln Lore,* no. 1665, November 1976.

Newman, Ralph G., ed. *Lincoln for the Ages.* New York: Doubleday, 1960.

Nicolay, John G. "Lincoln's Literary Experiments." *Century Magazine,* April 1894, 823–32.

Nicolay, John G., and John Hay. *Abraham Lincoln: A History.* 10 vols. New York: Century, 1917.

———, eds. *Abraham Lincoln: Collected Works.* 2 vols. New York: Century, 1894.

Paddock, Gaius. "Is the Sangamon River Navigable?" *Journal of the Illinois State Historical Society* 13, no. 1 (April 1920): 48–50.

Parkinson, Robert Henry. "The Patent Case That Lifted Lincoln into a Presidential Candidate." *Abraham Lincoln Quarterly* 4, no. 3 (September 1946): 105–22.

Poore, Benjamin Perley. "Lincoln and the Newspaper Correspondents." In Rice, *Reminisces of Abraham Lincoln,* 326–41.

Pratt, Harry, ed. *Concerning Mr. Lincoln.* Springfield, IL: Abraham Lincoln Association, 1944.

"President Elect's Mode of Buoying Vessels, The." *Scientific American,* December 1, 1860.

"Presidential Patent, A." *Harper's Weekly,* April 6, 1861, 210.

"President Lincoln as an Inventor." *Scientific American,* May 27, 1865.

"Recent American Decisions: In the Circuit Court of the United States, Northern District of Illinois, July term, 1855: Cyrus H. McCormick vs. John H. Manny, et al." *American Law Register* 4, no. 5 (March 1856): 277–93.

Rice, Allen Thorndike, ed. *Reminiscences of Abraham Lincoln by Distinguished Men of His Time.* Rev. ed. New York: Harper, 1909.

Riddle, Donald W. *Congressman Abraham Lincoln.* Urbana: University of Illinois Press, 1957.

Sandburg, Carl. *Lincoln Collector: The Story of Oliver R. Barrett's Great Private Collection.* New York: Harcourt, Brace, 1949.

Schneller, Robert J., Jr. *A Quest for Glory: A Biography of Rear Admiral John A Dahlgren*. Annapolis, MD: Naval Institute Press, 1996.

Stowell, Daniel W., ed. *The Papers of Abraham Lincoln: Legal Documents and Cases*. With the assistance of Susan Krause, John A. Lupton, Stacy Pratt McDermott, Christopher A. Schnell, and Dennis E. Suttles. 4 vols. Charlottesville: University of Virginia Press, 2008.

Swett, Leonard. "Lincoln's Story of His Own Life." In Rice, *Reminiscences of Abraham Lincoln*, 67–80.

Tarbell, Ida. *The Life of Abraham Lincoln*. 4 vols. New York: Lincoln History Society, 1908.

Temple, Wayne C. *Abraham Lincoln: From Skeptic to Prophet*. Mahomet, IL: Mayhaven, 1995.

———. "Herndon on Lincoln: An Unknown Interview with a List of Books in the Lincoln & Herndon Law Office." *Journal of the Illinois State Historical Society* 98, no. 1–2 (Spring–Summer 2005): 34–50.

———. *Lincoln's Connection with the Illinois & Michigan Canal, His Return from Congress in '48, and His Invention*. Springfield, IL: Illinois Bell, 1986.

———. "Lincoln the Lecturer, Part I." *Lincoln Herald* 101, no. 3 (Fall 1999): 94–110.

———. "Lincoln the Lecturer, Part II." *Lincoln Herald* 101, no. 4 (Winter 1999): 146–63.

Thomas, Benjamin P. Foreword. In *Lincoln and the Tools of War*, by Robert V. Bruce, vii–xi. Indianapolis, IN: Bobbs-Merrill, 1956.

Thomas, Benjamin P., and Harold M. Hyman. *Stanton: The Life and Times of Lincoln's Secretary of War*. New York: Knopf, 1962.

Townsend, George Alfred. *Washington, Outside and Inside: A Picture and a Narrative of the Origin, Growth, Excellences, Abuses, Beauties, and Personages of Our Governing City*. Hartford, CT: Betts, 1873.

Turner, Justin G. "Lincolniana: The Grimsley Trunk." *Journal of the Illinois State Historical Society* 66, no. 4 (Winter 1973): 455–59.

U.S. Congress. *Congressional Globe*. 46 vols. Washington, DC: 1834–73.

U.S. Constitution, art. 1, § 8, cl. 8.

U.S. Patent Office. *Report of the Commissioner of Patents, for the Year 1849*. 31st Congress, 1st Session, Ex. Doc. no. 20. Washington, DC: Office of Printers to House of Representatives, 1850.

"War and Inventions." *Scientific American*, May 25, 1861.

Weik, Jesse W. *The Real Lincoln: A Portrait*. Boston: Houghton Mifflin, 1922.

Welles, Gideon. *Diary of Gideon Welles: Secretary of the Navy under Lincoln and Johnson*. With an Introduction by John T. Morse Jr. 3 vols. Boston: Houghton Mifflin, 1911.

Whitney, Henry Clay. *Life on the Circuit with Lincoln*. Caldwell, ID: Caxton, 1940.

Wills, Garry. *Lincoln at Gettysburg: The Words That Remade America*. New York: Simon and Schuster, 1992.

Wilson, Douglas L., and Rodney O. Davis, eds. *Herndon's Informants: Letters, Interviews, and Statements about Abraham Lincoln*. Urbana: University of Illinois Press, 1998.

Wiltse, Charles M., ed. *The Papers of Daniel Webster*. Series 1: Correspondence. 7 vols. Hanover, NH: University Press of New England, 1984.

Zane, Charles S. "Lincoln as I Knew Him." *Sunset Magazine* 29, October 1912.

INDEX

Page numbers in italics indicate illustrations.

Jason Emerson is the author or editor of seven books about Abraham Lincoln and his family, including *The Madness of Mary Lincoln* and *Giant in the Shadows: The Life of Robert T. Lincoln*. He has published numerous articles and reviews in both scholarly and popular publications, and has appeared on The History Channel, H2, CNBC, Book TV, and American History TV. For more information, visit Jason's website at www.jasonemerson.com.

CONCISE
LINCOLN
LIBRARY

This series of concise books fills a need for short studies of the life, times, and legacy of President Abraham Lincoln. Each book gives readers the opportunity to quickly achieve basic knowledge of a Lincoln-related topic. These books bring fresh perspectives to well-known topics, investigate previously overlooked subjects, and explore in greater depth topics that have not yet received book-length treatment. For a complete list of titles, see www.conciselincolnlibrary.com.

Other Books in the Concise Lincoln Library

Abraham Lincoln and Horace Greeley
Gregory A. Borchard

Lincoln and the Civil War
Michael Burlingame

Lincoln's Sense of Humor
Richard Carwardine

Lincoln and the Constitution
Brian R. Dirck

Lincoln in Indiana
Brian R. Dirck

Lincoln and Native Americans
Michael S. Green

Lincoln and the Election of 1860
Michael S. Green

Lincoln and Congress
William C. Harris

Lincoln and the Union Governors
William C. Harris

Lincoln and the Abolitionists
Stanley Harrold

Lincoln's Campaign Biographies
Thomas A. Horrocks